AN OZARK ODYSSEY

AN OZARK ODYSSEY

THE JOURNEY OF A FATHER AND SON

WILLIAM CHILDRESS

Southern Illinois University Press
Carbondale

Library of Congress Cataloging-in-Publication Data
Childress, William.
  An Ozark odyssey : the journey of a father and son /
William Childress.
    p. cm.
    1. Childress, William. 2. Childress, William—Family.
3. Poets, American—20th century—Biography.
4. Migrant agricultural laborers—Ozark Mountains
Region. 5. Fathers and sons—Ozark Mountains
Region. 6. Ozark Mountains Region—Biography.
7. Childress, J. W., 1915–1997. I. Title.
  PS3553.H487Z47 2005
  811'.54—dc22
  ISBN 0-8093-2638-8 (cloth : alk. paper)
  ISBN 0-8093-2639-6 (pbk. : alk. paper)   2005000331

In memory of James Fullerton,
who never stopped trying

CONTENTS

PREFACE

AN EARLIER BOOK of mine, *Out of the Ozarks*, published in 1989, chronicled my life in the Ozark Mountains from 1973, when I arrived as a divorced father with three young sons, to 1984—the year I was nominated for a Pulitzer prize for my newspaper column in the *St. Louis Post-Dispatch*. This book, *An Ozark Odyssey*, explores the vagabond lives of the Childress family. J. W. Childress married my mother, Viola Lorraine Couch, and though he was my stepfather, he never let his guard down enough to let me know what was in his heart until we were far into our life's journey. He was the only father I ever knew. In their long years of marriage, the two of them raised me, a brother, and two sisters the best they knew how.

Our lives as a family were mostly spent in the Ozarks of Missouri, Arkansas, and Oklahoma, although as migrant workers we also lived in California, Arizona, and Texas, where we cut broomcorn, picked cotton, and took any farm jobs we could find. What schooling I had came from Oklahoma, Texas, Arizona, and California. We suffered bitter cold, scorpion-killing sun, and rich farmers who exploited us by paying as little as possible for our sweat while providing us with no medical care or other benefits. We lived in army tents or leaky shacks, freezing in winter and baking in summer. For the first seventeen years of my life, I never saw a doctor or a dentist. We were too poor. The first toothbrush I ever owned was given to me by the army, when I enlisted for the Korean War.

Our social status? Poor white trash.

Following the agrarian highway from east to west in an old truck, we harvested crops according to each state's weather pattern—which wasn't always the same. We could be picking cotton under a Texas sun, and suddenly a cold norther would rush in and wrap the cotton fields in icy gray mist. I often wondered what we would do if a tornado suddenly struck when we were out in the open with no shelter.

Oddly enough, that gypsy lifestyle prepared me for the profession I follow today. My dad never left the country he was born in, but as a travel writer and photographer, I've roamed the world. My wanderlust came from a variety of odysseys, some in hard circumstances, but I'm also indebted to stories from dad's own nomadic years. He was a teenage hobo, skilled at survival on the mean trains of the late 1920s and early 1930s. Once, when he was fifteen, another hobo tried to rape him in a boxcar. Dad, strong from farm labor, picked him up and threw him bodily from the moving train.

"You should've seen the bastard bounce," he told me many years later, in a rare talkative mood as we drank Acme beer under a big oak tree. The tree loomed near a dugout silo, and we were dressing the last hog we would ever butcher, re-creating our 1940s sharecropping experiences. A rope tied to a singletree, whose hooks threaded its hocks, passed through a pulley secured to a thick oak limb. We were scraping bristles off after immersing the carcass in a scalding barrel set over a crackling fire. To his dying day, dad hated the railroad industry and the bullies they hired to beat the hell out of kids who had done nothing but try to survive on their own when their parents could no longer feed them.

My mother and father were too different to have a graceful marriage, so they didn't. In general, dad was the silent type, while mom loved to talk. His quietness got under her skin and sometimes made her blow up. Her volubility sometimes made him desperate to get away.

"Why don't you just be a fence post?" she would yell. "Why don't you just do that?"

"Aw, hon," dad would say.

They could have blistering arguments at the slam of a screen door. Yet, somehow, they kept their fire-and-gunpowder marriage together for fifty-five years, giving us kids the greatest gift of all, their presence. They never avoided their family duties. They were firm believers in personal responsibility.

Dad was fond of saying, "People who talk about the good old days never lived where I did." He taught me the basics of life, not by pleading or lectures, but by telling me what to do and making sure I did it. To my three siblings and me, dad was godlike. His word was law, and when necessary, he enforced it.

The idea of parents bribing kids or begging them to behave did not sit well with him. He felt it created spoiled brats, extortionists, and future bullies. He also believed the children of baby boomers, when they became parents themselves, did not prepare their children for life's realities.

"The world ain't a nursery," he declared. "One way or another, people suffer pain and punishment, and parents ain't always there to soften the blows. Cops and employers ain't mom and dad, and kids who grow up with no respect for authority usually find themselves behind bars." He believed in properly designated authority but hated it when it derived from the power of money. He was also convinced that no society could survive by allowing citizens to do exactly as they pleased.

TODAY, MY PARENTS lie side by side in a country cemetery near Anderson, Missouri, the Ozark town they called home for the last thirty years of their lives. Their four children live far away—Glenda, Helen, and I in California, David in Idaho. We rarely visit their graves, but when we do, we always replace the plastic flowers my stepfather favored. "What good are real flowers on a grave?" he used to say. "These stay pretty longer."

Although we learned to accept the quarrels and shouting matches of our parents, we sure never liked them. One way or another, reconciliation would follow, but as the oldest, I sometimes had to get between them. I once took a butcher knife away from mom, who was using it to teach dad how to run.

In spite of such shenanigans, we knew our parents loved each other. Except for occasional separations, which may have helped their longevity, they were together until a brain tumor killed mom in 1992. Dad followed from emphysema five years later. Still, total forgiveness comes hard. Even though their own mental disarray may have been caused by the pain of their early lives, they created problems for us kids that we've battled against all our lives. In my more pessimistic moments, I revise John Dryden's three-hundred-year-old couplet for his dead wife, substituting my parents:

> Here lie my parents, here let them lie,
> Now they have peace, and so have I.

AN OZARK ODYSSEY

1

IT'S OCTOBER 1997, and I'm flying to the Ozarks. My fiddle-footed father is dead. The vagabond heart that took him the length and breadth of America is forever stilled. His mode of travel ranged from boxcars to shank's mare, but he never rode in an airplane in his life. "I ain't never going to ride one, neither," he declared, and in almost eighty-two years of life, he never did.

For some reason, the thought makes me tighten my seat belt. As the DC-10 wings towards the Ozarks and dad's funeral, I still hear John Dean, my brother-in-law, phoning me in Sacramento to tell me he's dead. After many years of living a mile from dad, of seeing him through heart sickness and heart surgery, I wasn't there when he died.

"His heart just gave out, Bill. I went over to his trailer to tell him breakfast was ready, and he was lying on the floor. His oxygen tank was on the bed." John's voice was full of sadness, but I felt no emotion. Deep down, I knew why. I was my father's son, or rather, my stepfather's stepson. I had learned as a child to keep my feelings under tight control, just as he had.

The call came on an ordinary day, and after I hung up, I was surprised to see just how ordinary it was. The sun was shining, an October breeze stirred the oleanders by the fence, and blue jays bickered in an orange tree. How could things feel so normal when the only man I ever called father was dead?

And he wasn't even my father. He was my stepfather.

DAD'S HEART HELD its share of kindness, but he had a temper, too. Still, he made it possible for me to have a father, and if he wasn't always the best, he was far from the worst I might have had. I'd been born out of wedlock, and few men are willing to take on a child that isn't theirs. Bastard births were real stigmas in 1933, particularly to Oklahoma Baptists.

An inner sadness kept dad from giving the approval or affection that meant so much to his kids. He was a stern parent, keeping a tight lid on his own feelings and having little patience with those who couldn't. But he was always there in our lives. He never abandoned his family, as so many men do. Sometimes he worked far away, hauling wheat in Montana and Canada to bring in money. But he always came home. And he always had at least a stick of hard candy for us kids.

He could have died in his forties when he had his first heart attack, just as his father had done. But thanks to Dr. John Graham, a fine Missouri cardiologist who performed a quintuple bypass on dad's heart when he was sixty-eight, his heart lasted nearly eighty-two years, beating some 2.5 billion times before stopping.

His father, George E. Rastus Childress, had died at the breakfast table at the age of forty-five. On a golden morning in 1922, he suddenly groaned and clutched his chest as a dying heart took him to eternity. Dad, who was just a little boy at the time, watched helplessly as three of the older sons, not knowing what else to do, massaged their father's feet and hands—to no avail.

Seventy years later, dad still remembered the menu: fried potatoes, ham, eggs, biscuits and gravy, jelly, and butter. At seven years of age, he only knew that his father was gone forever. He stayed close to his pregnant mother, a stoic and solemn little boy unable to comprehend the vastness of his loss and too young to fathom the financial problems that would befall the family.

Six weeks after her husband's funeral, Sudie Childress died following the birth of her ninth child, Jack. She was forty-three years of age when blood poisoning, almost certainly caused by the unclean hands of a country doctor, took her life. "Nothin' in the world killed my mother but an old country doctor's filthy hands," dad told me. "He wasn't no good, but he was all we had. He liked his whiskey too much."

Dad became attached to the new baby with an intensity that lasted his whole life. Little did he know, then, that Jack, the squirming infant in the crib, would grow up to endure and survive some of the most terrifying battles of the D-day invasion—and that, for most of his life, he would feel guilt over the death of the mother he never knew.

When dad's mom died of septicemia, or perhaps childbed fever, there were nine children—seven boys and two girls. The second death in less than two months struck the family like a bomb. The older brothers buried their mother beside their father in Navahoe Cemetery, out on an open plain, and then decided the fate of the kids who were still small. The death of their parents meant the younger siblings had to be parceled out among the older ones, several of whom were already grown and starting farms of their own. These were Guy, the oldest, then Hamp, then Bid, and finally Tom. The assets of the farm were divided up, and the Childresses went back to the labor of living.

IN MY FILES in California, there's a picture of dad that I discovered among mom's old photographs. It's my favorite image of the crusty, withdrawn, sometimes selfish man who agreed to be my father and did his best to steer me around life's shoals.

The picture shows a kid of perhaps eight or nine standing at the end of a bridge. It was taken in the early 1920s, and the boy's face is shaded by the bill of his too-big cap, the kind worn by James Cagney in his hoodlum movies. He's standing straight, looking at the camera, one trouser leg rolled above his knee, the other to mid-shin. It's both an endearing picture of a little boy and a mystery. His shadowed face represents the man I never got to know, the man who kept everything inside, including the deaths of his own parents when he was seven.

It's impossible to imagine the shock his dad's dying must have had on my father as he sat at the table, watching it happen—only to be followed a few weeks later by the death of his mother. Two tragedies, coming so close together, helped make my dad silent, distant, and sometimes cold—although basically he was a kind man. The trauma had to be lifelong, but he never complained about any part of his life. Up to the very end, he remained a stoic, taciturn patriarch, knowing that his kids, raised under that curious banner, would always come to him. We had to. He never came to us.

At seven, dad and his younger sister Jo, who was four, were sent to live with Hamp, who was in his late twenties, and his ultrareligious wife—as quick with a leather belt as she was with one of her wild, hand-wriggling prayers. Fear of hellfire and damnation made that woman mean. It always amazed me that, until she died at an advanced age, still clutching her Bible, dad treated her with every consideration—even though I knew that privately he couldn't stand her. Although she never had any children of her own, she had been his surrogate mother and was his brother's wife, and dad always had old-fashioned priorities.

Growing up, he buried his bleak and parentless childhood deep inside himself. But those tragedies, and his years on the road, hardened him beyond measure. The picture of him by the river bridge is the most gentle and sensitive ever taken, and it marked the end of whatever childhood he had. Less than five years later, at fourteen, unable to live with his brother's fanatical wife any longer, he would leave home and start riding the rails. Hunger, cold, and danger were his steady companions during those years.

"The way it happened," he told me, "was that one day Jo did something or other—it wasn't much—and that old woman grabbed a belt and was going to whip her. I couldn't take that, and I ran at her and yanked the belt out of her hand and told her if she ever tried to whip Jo again, I'd find out and fix her good. An hour later, I was in a boxcar and headed west."

A tramp at fourteen, my future stepfather wouldn't return home for seven years—and then not to stay. In fact, he would be a fiddlefoot for the rest of his life and would take his family along that selfsame path.

Mind you, I'm not complaining. Being on the road so much, as both child and adult, was a major part of my own education and taught me a degree of self-reliance I'd never have gotten elsewhere. At fifteen, sick to death of picking cotton, I ran away myself. (And yet, many years later, when one of my own sons talked about running away, it scared me to death.) Whoever said travel is broadening knew what they were talking about. It may not always be fun, and it can easily be dangerous, but it's always an education.

My father held many jobs, but he never held any of them for long—not even the good ones. He worked at farming the longest, although he never had much talent for it. And it seems like my leaving the farm to join the army gave him permission to admit to himself that he lacked agrarian ability. I would almost bet he told himself, "I'll be damned, I guess I *don't* have any talent for farming! And with Bill gone, I'm only half as interested. Reckon it's time for a change."

So he trained to be a plumber and a pipe fitter, both of which he did have talent for. He made good money until he retired years later—money that bought him his final Missouri farm. By then, though, he was too old for row cropping, so he began raising beef cattle. And darned if he didn't have talent for that, too!

Dad was almost fifty-five before he found his niche in life, but when he did, he made up for lost time. Here was a man who never completed high school, yet when he died, to our astonishment, he had taken care of all the funeral needs of mom and himself. Even more amazing, he was able to give each kid $25,000 in his will. Pretty good for an ex-migrant worker and sharecropper.

That doesn't mean he was a saint. He had a temper and a heavy hand sometimes and could even be a little cruel—like the day we were fixing an electric fence, and he told me to put both hands on it to see whether it was working. It was, and my elbows took off for parts unknown.

He was also, frankly, a bigot. Not an evil one—he would do no one harm—but he refused to associate with black people his whole life except in the cotton fields, where ethnic groups worked side by side. But he wouldn't speak to them there, and he widened his bias to include Latinos, Orientals, and "queers," as he called gay people—all of which he owed to his Oklahoma upbringing. He never did anything to them; he simply avoided them.

He also thought a woman's place was in the home, preferably pregnant. In later years, mom used the fact that he had given her three kids in twenty-nine months as the basis for one or more of her wars against him. "I was surrounded by diapers and squawling all through 1938 and 1939," mom said, "and when Helen come along in 1941, the other two was just big enough to dig out all the poison they could find and give theirselves a tonic."

Throughout his life, dad was embarrassed to show his emotions. No, not embarrassed, *ashamed.* Strong men weren't supposed to be emotional. He was afraid of affection, to give it or receive it, and that was hard on mom. She came from a loveless, deranged family herself, and we kids knew she needed more love and affection from dad than he could ever give her. If you mistrust affection, you can build resistance to emotional pain. Dad believed a man should be stoic and uncomplaining, and that's what he was. It was his best defense. *If you're wounded, don't show it:* that was his philosophy.

When I was in the army, I got word that he'd had a serious heart attack and, although he was still relatively young at forty-two, might not make it. I got a short furlough and rushed home. He was out of danger when I got there, but so great was my relief, I forgot myself and tried to hug him. He shoved me rudely away, and never again did we touch in any emotional context. Only after he became an old man, and I an almost-old one, would he allow me or my brother, David, to hug him, although it was different with the girls, especially his first-born, Glenda, who was spoiled rotten by him.

THE PLANE'S PASSENGERS fade away, and dad's lean form and weathered face take shape in my mind. He's five feet eleven, weighs one hundred sixty pounds, is clad in overalls, and smells of sweat, tobacco, and alfalfa. He speaks in a deep, rumbling voice, and his blue eyes are framed by coal-black hair that will still be free of gray when he's eighty. Physically, he's the archetypal small farmer and field worker, which is what he's been for most of his life. Although he was the only father I ever knew, I didn't always appreciate him back then.

My brother-in-law John and sister Helen were Californians, but when dad reached seventy-seven, they bought a summer trailer on Oklahoma's Grand Lake, also known as Grand Lake o' the Chero-kees, next door to his. He had sold his Missouri farm and retired to the state he'd been born in.

I never understood his attachment to Oklahoma. But that's where he was born, and that's where he died. I was born there too, but Oklahoma didn't like me, and I didn't like it.

As dad aged, both Helen and Glenda took their vacations near him, often coming when travel assignments took me away. Helen and her husband, John, were visiting when dad died, and even though he died alone, he knew some of his family was near—a blessing not everyone receives.

IN A FEW HOURS, I'd be meeting my brother and sisters—David, Glenda, and Helen. We were half siblings, but we never thought of it that way. This would mark the first time in years we'd all been together, facing what every family faces when death comes calling.

Not that dad was really dead, or mom either, in my mind. They were as sharp and clear in my memory as painted portraits. People with personalities as strong as theirs are hard to forget, and as long as they exist in my heart, they're immortal. I could even hear the old man's grumbly baritone when I asked him, after he turned sev-enty, if he ever thought about dying.

"What kind of damn fool question is that?" he snapped.

"Well, *I* think about it," I said defensively. "Everybody dies, you know."

"Everybody don't go around talking about it."

Later, he admitted he did think about it. He didn't put much stock in religion, saying he'd simply tried to live his life the best he knew how. If there was a God, which he personally doubted, then

God should take the way he'd lived his life into account without a lot of breast-beating and praying.

"The silly asses," he said, speaking of churchgoers. "They pray, all right, but look at the wars they get into."

BOTH OF OUR PARENTS came from hard, painful childhoods, where root, hog, or die was the fundamental law. Dad was a small boy when he lost both his father and his mother, being raised thereafter by kinfolks. It did a lot to drain the well of his emotions. Mom endured an ignorant, abusive father, whom she hated to her dying day, and who actually impregnated one of his daughters. That cruel and ignorant Texan fathered seventeen children, ignored them until they were big enough to work, and then worked them like mules, regularly beating the hell out of them. More than once I've thought it would be nice if hell actually did exist, just so he could sizzle there until he was a little black lump of charcoal. I am ashamed that he really was my grandfather. Suffice it to say, mom's feelings about her father colored her feelings about all men. She didn't even go to his funeral when he died in a car wreck in Dallas in 1937.

My blood father met my mother at a country dance and whirled her out into the moonlight. He must have been some dancer, because nine months later, I waltzed into the world. By that time, dear old dad had vanished like the mist, so mom raised me by herself, working at any job she could get, from chopping wood to sewing canvas army tents.

I have a picture of her that shows a pretty young woman with finger-waved hair, looking down at a moon-faced baby in her arms. There is a kind of wonder in her face. How odd it seems, being so far removed from that infant and that time.

I never knew I was born out of wedlock until I was thirteen, and even then I was so backward I didn't really understand what mom was telling me. Small wonder. Our folks never told us anything about sexual reproduction. Most of our "sex ed" came from schoolmates or from the little comic books that found their way into our grade schools in the 1940s.

As an example, in 1947 there was a movie called *Mom and Dad,* which showed the actual birth of a baby. This revolutionary film (it toured the country for decades) was aimed at teenagers, but if other parents were like ours, no teenage kids saw it. That was when we lived on the old Charlie Pokero place in Oklahoma for the second time, dad being a glutton for punishment. I wanted to see *Mom and Dad,* because it was stated over the airwaves that this movie was one that all parents should attend with any of their kids who were twelve or over, and I was pushing fourteen.

"You don't have no business seein' that movie," dad growled. Mom agreed with him—one of the few times she did, I might add. Instead, *they* went to see it! Afterwards, they didn't tell us a blessed thing. Of course, given the sexual ignorance of our parents, the movie was probably a real shocker for them.

Anyway, mom and I were hoeing weeds out of some hilltop corn, where the stalks were half the size of those raised in rich bottom-land soil. Wind swirled the dust around us like red fog, and suddenly, aggravated beyond endurance, I shouted, "Damn this wind!"

That was strong language for a kid of thirteen in 1946. Mom got fire in her eyes, threw down her hoe, and said, "Don't you *ever* let me hear you say that again! That's God's wind, and he can do anything he wants to with it!" I don't even remember what brought it up, but a moment later she was talking in slow, measured, confessional tones about how I had come to be. I was, after all, light complexioned (I'm a Dane), while dad had dark hair and was dark complexioned.

Mom told me my real father's name, and how he had promised to marry her, and how his mother had been an iron-pants bitch who kept him firmly in check—or in checks, since mom indicated that my blood father's family was wealthy. Who knows how much it hurt her to reveal that she had fallen from grace and that I, a clumsy little kid, was the result?

I didn't know what mom was talking about back then, because I was dumber than a turnip. But she had endured the fact of others knowing it, and her shame gradually made her hard to live with.

When her demons seized her, she said some harsh things to me, but she also loved me the best she knew how. I owed my life to her twice—once when she gave birth to me, and once when she saved me from a fire set by an arsonist.

As for dad, he once saved me from a charging steer, demolishing his brand-new .410 shotgun, which he used as a club to knock the animal down. But it couldn't have been easy for him to take on and raise a four-year-old who obviously wasn't his kid. However, he never took the easy way out by telling people I was his stepson. Once when I was on leave from the army, blond haired, blue eyed, and square jawed, dad took me to a bar for a beer where there was a dreary jerk with pig eyes and a nose that someone had previously rearranged. He and dad exchanged a few noncommittal words, and then he asked, "That yer kid?"

"Yep," my old man said, and I glowed inside.

The guy stared at me. I stared back harder at him. I was just out of paratrooper training and filled out my uniform pretty good. If he wanted a tussle, he'd get one.

The fool kept on. "Is he *sure enough* yer kid?" he demanded, with an odd look in his eyes.

Dad turned and hit him with a cold stare. "I told you yes," he said quietly. "Now why don't you blow?"

The guy blew.

Illegitimacy, however, was a terrible sin to most folks in 1933, and in Hugo, Oklahoma, where mom was living before she met dad, the good Southern Baptist churchgoers regarded sexual misdeeds with all the generosity of rattlesnakes. Mom soon left for Texas, because somehow those folks forgot that to err is human, to forgive divine, if they ever knew it.

IT WAS A June day in 1936. I see it all in my mind's eye: The Texas earth was sunbaked and parched, with cracks as wide as shovel handles in the yellow surface. Even the trees in the nearby pine forest were painted with dust. The sound of crows echoed from the dense woods, while buzzards floated upwards as though pulled by invisible wires. An ancient, two-story gray house stood on a knoll, with a rickety log barn leaning perilously towards it. A long-dead tree at one corner lifted its gray bones to the sky. Mom, dressed in a pretty red dress, her coppery hair newly finger-waved, was preparing to go someplace. She had lost her dollar-a-day job at the tent factory and was leaving me with her sister and brother and heading for a place called Arizona to find work. Years later, she would say, "Things was so bad at that tent factory job, it was the next thing to no job at all."

At three and a half, I didn't understand much of what was going on, except that everybody seemed excited. I can picture mom and her sister Neva chattering while her sister's husband, John, stood around. Nothing much ever happened in their lives but plowing, planting, and gathering their meager crops.

"Oh, honey," my aunt said. "Are you sure you'll be all right? It's such a long trip on that ol' Greyhound bus!"

"I'll be fine, sis," mom said. "You just take good care of my baby boy."

"Oh, I will, I will! He's like one of our'n, you know that." She and mom hugged.

"Best come on, Lorraine," I can hear my uncle saying. "This old Ford don't go very fast. Got your bus ticket?"

Mom waved a slip of green paper, then smiled and leaned down to kiss me good-bye. "You be good, now," she said, as her brother-in-law gave the Ford's crank a rapid spin. The motor chuckled into life with the cheery sound a Model T makes, and with draperies of dust rippling behind them, they were gone.

My long-nosed aunt never questioned the idea that my mom was looking for work, but she was closer to the truth when she said, "Your mama is going to try and find you a daddy!" That was fine with me, as I guessed I could use one. There were missing daddies in 1937, too, but since I'd never had a daddy, I didn't know much about what one did. My cousins, who were both older than me, seemed to have one who took them out to the woodshed now and then, which didn't interest me.

IT WOULD BE YEARS before I found out that my future stepfather had been in the army in San Antonio, Texas, and didn't like either the army or Texas. So he petitioned to buy his way out, which was legal then, and his brother Hamp loaned him the money to buy his way out. But he didn't like the idea of a cold boxcar trip back to Oklahoma, so he decided to head for Arizona.

"They had a travelers' column in the San Antonio newspaper that posted ads for rides," he told me, "so I contacted a guy who owned a La Salle, a pretty fancy car back then, and paid him. He had five passengers—three other men, a nice-looking woman, and me. Her and me got along real good from the start.

"But I reckon the driver had eyes for her, too, and hoped to get her to like him. She was blond, blue-eyed, and had a nice figure and said she hadn't met a man like me, who was black-haired but had blue eyes like hers.

"She wouldn't give that driver the time of day, though, so that evening in an El Paso café, he pretended he had left his wallet in the car and went to get it. Then he took off for L.A., leaving all five of us stranded in El Paso.

"The woman had some folks in Bisbee, so her and me took a bus there and stayed with her sister and husband for a day. Then she went her way, and I went mine. It was unusual for women to travel alone in those days, but she did all right. She was a tall, pretty woman, twenty-four to my twenty-one." Dad frowned. "I can't call up her name," he said, "but if she's still alive, she's pretty old today. Funny how you remember stuff like that."

The idea of my dad "going his way" from a pretty woman who liked him is almost certainly poppycock. He was never one to boast about it, but women found him attractive, and he committed more than a few adulteries during his life. One reliable source caught him in bed with an attractive Danish girl in her twenties. He was about sixty at the time.

During one of my parents' separations that lasted a few months (when we kids were grown and settled elsewhere), he chose the wrong woman—an Arkansas gal who bedded him, saw him slip his money in his boot, and when he was asleep, slipped it right out again. That was the last he saw of her or the $1,500 she stole.

"She sure wasn't worth no fifteen hundred in bed," he said later.

Once he gave mom an unwanted "gift" from some other lady that almost broke up their marriage. "The bastard gave me the crabs," mom said, madder than a rooster in a Mexican cockfight. She had never been so factual with me before. But somehow, the old man talked his way out of that one, too, perhaps by suggesting she got them from a toilet lid.

AFTER DAD LEFT the blond, he rode all day with a star route postman to Nogales, where his brother Bid was working on a dairy. Within a week, Bid quit his job, and the two headed for Phoenix. They were skilled hand-milkers, so a job on an Italian dairy soon followed—John Masera was the owner's name. But dad and Bid were footloose and fancy free, and they soon took off for Mesa, Arizona.

During the Depression, the secret to having a job was to have a skill or talent that someone needed. In the 1930s, when milking machines were still new and largely mistrusted, hand-milkers were in demand. As it turned out, mom and dad were now in the same area, and fate was making it possible for them to meet. Before they did meet, though, his brother Bid took off for Oklahoma. Dad said Bid was simply homesick, and that was that.

"It was about six months after Bid left that I met your mother," dad was saying. He was in his favorite chair, in the trailer, with his Siamese cat Si-Si on his lap. The big picture window looked out on Grand Lake. So did Si-Si, for she was interested in a tribe of birds bathing at the water's edge.

Dad never liked cats until he passed middle age, but over the past couple of decades, he had grown more tolerant, even about the wild ones living in his barn during the years when he was still farming. Sometimes he put food out for them, but only in winter. "Never give 'em too much," he cautioned. "If a cat ain't hungry, she won't catch rats." His advice excluded the Siamese, who was spoiled rotten and the apple of his eye. Si-Si would have run from any rat she encountered.

"Back in 1936, I won a 1931 Model A Ford in a raffle," dad went on. "A black one with a rumble seat." (I loved riding in that rumble seat and I'm glad modern car makers are reinventing them). "So, I was feeling pretty cocky. The car was five years old, but it ran real good, which was all I cared about.

"I won it from one of the brothers of a family named LaBell, who lived in cotton pickers' shacks and picked cotton to survive. For awhile, I went with one of the LaBell girls—she would come and get me for dances or picnics. One night she brought Lorraine with her, and it just went on from there."

Dad stopped talking every so often, as though collecting his thoughts, but he was probably reliving those days when he was young and strong and hadn't a care in the world. Why should he? He was single, with his own car, had no trouble getting jobs or girls, and had money in his pocket at a time when sixteen million people were out of work, thanks to the Republicans.

"After about a month, Lorraine said if I saw that LaBell girl again, she—Lorraine—wouldn't have nothing more to do with me. I was pretty well hooked and netted by then, anyway, and your mom was redheaded and pretty, so I didn't mind. Not long afterward, she told me she had a little boy back in Texas—that being you. She asked me if that mattered, and I said no.

"So we went to a justice of the peace, got married, and moved to Mesa, Arizona, to a four-room white house surrounded by some orange trees. That's where your sister, Glenda, was born."

A shadow came over his face. He was telling this particular anecdote in the mid-1980s, after mom had divorced him and moved out. Then in her early seventies, mom would stay gone two years, living in senior housing and slowly becoming a local barfly.

Finally, my father added sadly, "Your mother was a different person when she was a young woman."

BISCUITS OF CLOUDS sail past the plane's windows, allowing glimpses of the patchwork quilt below. Ozark autumns range from rusty brown through a vivid range of colors, and every year, like a pointillist's dream, the earth under the trees is sprinkled with broken rainbows.

It would be good to stroll through the woods I'd roamed for over two decades, but the thought brought me no joy. No longer could I walk into my parents' yard and see them working in their garden, or feeding the clucking, silly old Domineckers and Buff Orphingtons they kept as pets for so many years, or be a reluctant referee at one of their quarrels.

My wife, Diane, had recently surprised me by framing a full-page photo of mom from a 1977 farm magazine's cover. There she stood, surrounded by rows of quart jars filled with tomatoes, pickles, and peaches. It's a great picture of her when she was still mom, and not the unhappy woman she became. Her skill at canning kept us fed through many a hard winter.

Mom was a big woman, two hundred and forty pounds on a five-foot-four frame, and yet she could bend over and touch the earth with her palms. I've never been able to touch my toes, not even when I was a bone-hard paratrooper. I still can't, and dad never bothered to try. But all his life, he escaped arthritis, while mom and I didn't. It's in the genes, I guess, and his aren't mine.

I FIRST SAW J. W. Childress, the man who became my father, in the summer of 1938, in Mesa, Arizona—nine years after he left the Oklahoma Ozarks as a teenage hobo on a freight train. He was twenty-two, mom was three years older, and I was four and change.

Half a century later, he would tell me, "In 1929, when I hit the road, there wasn't nothin' unusual about bein' a tramp. They was lots of kids riding the rails, all over the country. Most of their families had no jobs and couldn't feed 'em, so they wasn't much they could do but head for the horizon.

"Today, when kids disappear, all kinds of attempts are made far and wide to locate them. But in those days, nobody knew or cared about the thousands of teenagers riding the rails. Nobody knows how many lie in unknown graves or became food for coyotes and wolves.

"It was a dangerous life, and we learned to be quick and run fast or get our heads knocked off by the railroad bulls—bastards hired by the goddamn railroads to beat our brains out with rubber truncheons if they caught us near the boxcars."

Dad told me about the time several hoboes were accidentally locked in a boxcar. The car was coupled to an engine and left on a desert siding for weeks. "When they finally hauled it back to the yards and opened it," he said, "wasn't nothin' left but bones and a bad smell."

When word of mom's marriage reached Texas, where I'd lived with kinfolks for more than a year, all of them were happy. My aunt showed the letter around that said mom wanted me with her, and one summer day two women I'd never seen appeared out of nowhere to take me to Arizona. Much later, I'd learn that one of them was Lola, mom's youngest sister, brown-haired and bubbly. She would be that way most of her life, until she died of cancer in a hospital room. One day just before she died, hysterical with fear, she threw her Bible across the room. She'd been raised in a religion that preached Bible miracles and the laying on of hands, but it hadn't cured her cancer like she'd hoped.

The other woman was Lola's friend Billie, who slipped a nickel into my hand and said, "We come to get you, sugarpie. We're gonna take you to Arizona, where your mama is waitin' with your new daddy." It had been over a year since I'd seen my mother. It was hard to recall what she looked like, because all I ever heard about her came in occasional letters sent to the long-nosed Texas aunt I stayed with. "Be sure and give my little boy lots of love" was the way the letters always ended, and mom always included a few dollars.

In general, though, I was pretty much ignored by the family, although my two cousins—both of them teenagers—played some mean tricks on me when I was three years old. Once they hid the chamber pot under a cardboard box with a weak bottom and then hollered, "Run and jump on it, Billy! It's fun!" I did, and went straight down into a couple of gallons of pee, Garrett snuff spit, and doo-doo.

When my aunt saw my soggy brown feet coming through the door, she was apoplectic with anger, switched both boys on their bare legs with a willow wand, and locked them in the woodshed. Those two must have known they would get their rear ends heated up when their father got back from town, and sure enough, I heard their yowls coming from the woodshed later.

FROM THE AGE of four and a half, you don't remember a lot of things, but I recall sitting in the back seat as Lola or Billie drove. The trip was very long, and I spent a lot of time sleeping. All I remember with any clarity was an enormous opening in the earth where Lola and Billie and I got out of the car and looked down into it. They chattered about what a "grand canyon" it was, but I didn't understand those words. It scared the hell out of me, even though both women held my hands as they walked me to the edge. "It's a whole mile to the bottom!" my aunt said. I didn't understand that, either. I just knew I was terrified.

One day, after a long journey through mountains and across parched desert, with searing air pouring through rolled-down windows, Aunt Lola's car thumped across some railroad tracks, and there we were in Mesa, Arizona. In 1938, it was a tiny little desert burg existing only for agriculture. (Sixty years later, it had close to three hundred thousand people.)

Occasionally studying a piece of paper in her hand, Aunt Lola finally pulled the dusty car into a gravel drive flanked by dark green trees. "*Orange* trees, Billy!" she told me excitedly. "See? Those little round green things are oranges. They're not ripe yet. They don't get ripe till December."

Then the door opened, and mom was pulling me out, hugging and kissing me, a big smile on her face. Behind her was a slender man with black hair. He had blue eyes and was wearing a white Stetson. From the side, his face looked like the face on the Indian head nickel Billie had given me. He wore jeans and a red plaid shirt.

Mom seemed fatter than when she'd left me with her Texas kin-folks, which for some reason brought giggles and more excited chatter from Billie and Lola.

"Well, Lorraine, when are you due?" they demanded, and mom said, "October—about four months." My new father and I were still sizing each other up, but then we all went into the house. There, gleaming in the cool dimness, was a red wagon. Except for a windup Caterpillar tractor with rubber treads given to me when I was two, it was the first new toy I'd ever had, and wouldn't you know, it would get me in trouble.

There were two houses in the orange grove, both of them small and white. A rarely seen young couple with a female dachshund lived in the one behind us, and a gravel road ran directly in front of ours. Cars raced up and down the road, and almost immediately my stepfather told me I must always stay in the yard and out of the road.

"You might get hit," he said. "Those cars would run right over you. So stay out of the road."

A week later, busy playing with the wagon, I forgot all about the road and was practically in the middle of it when I felt myself snatched up, and several hard spanks landed on my bottom. It hurt and scared me, as did the grim face of my brand-new father. "I told you about that road," he said. "You got to learn to listen to me!"

I could only sob, and not just for the spanking but because he had shocked me into peeing in my pants. For many years, I was mad at him for that spanking, which I considered unjust. One day, many years later, I brought it up during a visit, asking why he'd done it. That's when he told me about the road—a road I had long since forgotten.

"I was *in* the damn yard."

"No, you wasn't, neither. I wouldn't have spanked you for bein' in the yard."

There would be quite a bit of corporal punishment in my child-hood, some fair, some unfair, but writing these words just now reminded me of another time, much later, when dad was only a few years from death. We had walked out in the pasture and were looking at his herd. We each had a beer in our hands. He leaned back against a creep feeder and said, "I ain't never told you this, but I never made no difference between you and the other kids. I cared for you like I cared for them. I know there've been times when you thought I was wrong as wrong could be, and I can't change that. I tried to do the best I could."

He must have felt it wasn't always his best, though. Shortly before he died, he gave each of us a cash gift. But here, too, he let me know who was boss. He mailed my siblings theirs, but in true J. W. Childress fashion, said I'd have to collect mine in person. It was his way of saying that no matter what happened, I was still the oldest son and still had to do what he said.

"Maybe this will pay for some of that cotton you picked," he told me, handing me a $10,000 check. It was an ordinary bank-book check, made out in his impossibly scrawly hand.

"The bank won't cash that," I said.

"Why the hell not?"

"Because nobody can read your writing."

This time, he was ahead of me. "Okay, then, give it back."

I could tell he was proud of being able to do that for his kids, though, and he had every right to be. He may only have had a tenth-grade education in school, but he had a master's degree in life.

AUNT LOLA and Billie left, finally, and life settled into a routine that meant play for me and dairy work for dad. He was a hand-milker at a large, nearby dairy—I think it was called Kibbler's. Once he took me with him and gave me a shovel so big I could barely push it down the gutters that ran behind each stanchioned cow. The barn smelled acrid from urine and manure. After milking seventy-five cows (there was no such thing as an eight-hour day—jobs were too scarce), dad had to shovel out the manure and wash down the floors with a water hose. It didn't take me long to tire of the animals and the barn, and I never went back.

Mom kept getting fatter, and one day dad drove his Model A to the bus station and came home with a white-haired old lady who was even fatter than mom. I had not seen my grandma since I was a toddler of two, and it was awhile before I recognized her. She was there, my new dad said, to help my mom. Help her with what? my five-year-old mind asked. A month later, I had the answer: to help her bring home a squalling, red-faced baby—my first sister, Glenda.

It's hard to see her as she is today and remember her as that yowling little baby. Boy, could she holler! She had lungs like a fireplace bellows but would always be the apple of her daddy's eye. However, since she cried at night, and her daddy had to get up at 3:00 AM to start milking the cows (averaging ten cows an hour), he sometimes saw her as a sour apple.

Strange as it would later seem, but certainly through no fault of hers, my sister's birth marked the beginning of hard times and near tragedies for our family. Within weeks of bringing her home, mom cut her foot down to the bone on a broken Coke bottle while swimming in a Mesa canal. I still remember the deep, awful gash, like a red mouth, and how scared I was as dark blood welled up, staining the water. God, it was an ugly wound. A doctor stitched it, but mom couldn't put any weight on it for two weeks.

Even with grandma there, mom's disability meant extra duty for my stepfather, who couldn't help getting frustrated and irritable. One day he and mom exchanged angry words for the first time, and the little house rang with their yells. That made Glenda cut loose with one of her patented screeches, so mom and dad calmed down.

To add to their woes, the dairy where dad worked was sold, and he lost his job. It was November 1938. The Great Depression was running over us again.

As for grandma, who had given birth to seventeen children and known only the hardest of lives, she would soon be dead from cancer.

DAD AND MOM were both born along the edge of the Oklahoma Ozarks, in the southeastern part of the state. Raised on poor farms, a hardscrabble life was all they ever knew when they were kids.

Many years later, especially after he lost his chief mule (me) to the army, dad became a plumber. But farming was always in his blood, and in 1962 he returned to it. Toward the end of his life, he had acquired a good-sized herd of cows, so he quit row cropping. When it came time to retire, it broke his heart to see his cows auctioned off. They were so much like pets, he had named most of them, including Buster the Bull. I used to hear him crooning to them as I walked across the pasture from my house to his. Mom accused him of loving his cows more than he loved his family, which wasn't totally true, but there was competition. Cows don't have razor sharp tongues that can flay a person alive.

Dad once observed, "A woman's tongue is the sharpest weapon in the world—and she don't even know how crazy it can make a man." Cows were silent, and dad appreciated silence. Of course, that aggravated mom, who accused him of being abnormal.

"It's ab*nor*mal for anybody to be quiet for so long!" she complained more than once, trying out the new word she'd learned from some romance magazine. (Mom always read confessions, dad always read westerns. All he ever said about my first book, *Out of the Ozarks*, was, "I read the parts that wasn't exaggerated.")

As for my poor mother, her world was simple in her later years. All it required was for everyone to agree with whatever she said. The only person this didn't work for was dad. He agreed with her a lot, but to mom, that only meant he was hiding something.

"I'd like to know what that man is hiding!" she would say, her lips pressed grimly together. Sometimes she went to investigate and found dad talking to his cows, looking at his cows, or simply enjoying the silence with his cows. To mom, he was a wooden man without emotions. To my dad, mom was a volatile woman with nothing *but* emotions. It was the eternal battle of the sexes, multiplied by their hard childhoods, and in mom's case, the abusiveness of her sadistic and worthless father. Her hidden demons, planted by her tyrannical father when she was still small, would come roaring forth and inhabit her mind in later years, and the results would be melancholy, indeed.

But mom and dad's first year together was fairly idyllic—before a lack of jobs and money, plus a newborn baby and a five-year-old, brought the first of fifty-five years of strife—some of it as active as anything offered by a prize fight.

WHEN DAD LOST his job in Mesa, it was mid-September, and we had to move—but there was no place to move to. Then a friend of his told him that Taylorsville, a little out-of-the-way town in California's Sierra Mountain Range, had two dairies, and both needed milkers. My old man was never lazy—he secured *both* jobs, persuading the dairy owners that he had two of the best hands in the business. He did, too, for he had grown up milking cows. Clear into old age, he had a grip that could make a weight lifter wince.

In the waning days of the Great Depression, the world was rushing toward war. But my dad's chief concern was the family he had to support. He got $76 a month for sixteen hours a day, seven days a week. "Cows don't recognize holidays," he said.

The hardest part for him was getting up at 1:00 AM to start the milking. The barns were drafty, unheated and bitterly cold, and he never finished before 8:30 in the morning. His only warmth came from the cows themselves as he hunkered into their flanks and began emptying their udders. Then another eight-hour cycle started at 1:00 PM that lasted till 9:00 at night. Then he could sleep until 1:00 the next morning.

Dad never complained. His pay was good, although he worked double shifts for it, and a dollar in those days bought a lot of groceries. Many people were worse off, some of them showing up at the cabin's door, where mom gave them leftover biscuits or whatever she had. She hadn't forgotten about dad's own days as a hobo.

There were some fringe benefits—the two-room cabin rent-free and all the milk his family could use. Taylorsville even had its own creamery (still standing but no longer in use) that made ice cream, and dad sometimes brought home a brick of Neapolitan.

IF IT HADN'T BEEN common in those lean days to see people come and go, our family would have presented an odd picture to Taylorsvillians. A dilapidated homemade trailer wobbled behind the Hudson sedan dad had traded the Model A for, piled high with our few belongings.

The house was crudely furnished with a table, chairs, and bedstead, but mom had her own bedding, dishes, and other utensils necessary to make a home. A hard worker to the point of compulsion, she flew in and scrubbed the shack from top to bottom, using bleach and Lysol liberally, stopping now and then to breast-feed Glenda who, the rest of the time, watched owl-eyed and round-faced from her cardboard-box crib. She couldn't yet walk, but by holding the edges of the box, she could stand up, peer over, and gaze at the world around her.

I started school right away, trudging across the one-lane gravel road toward the flagpole centered in the schoolyard. Behind it, fortlike, stood the red-brick school with its pyramidal tin roof and small white portico.

The flapping of the flag matched the thudding of my heart, because this was a whole new game, and I wasn't sure how it was played. One teacher taught eight grades, all subjects, and she—meaning the late Mrs. Eldred—was like the captain of a ship. Her word was absolute law, and no parent would dream of marching to school to defend their kid. They probably would've been tossed through a window by Mrs. Eldred.

Dad milked in freezing barns, wearing a cumbersome coat and rubber boots. He was fast and sure, milking and stripping a cow (he told me years later) in about six minutes. Roughly three minutes per cow was needed to stanchion them for milking and to pour the foaming milk into a large cauldron from whence it went directly to the refrigerator.

But he lost weight from the sixteen-hour days, and his hands were always swollen and red. Sometimes at night, from my cot in the back of the cabin, I heard him and mom talking in low tones, measuring the worth of where they were against the possibility of something better elsewhere. Or maybe his fiddle-feet were just itching again. Before winter returned, dad told his employers he wanted his second baby—my brother David—to be born in a warmer clime, and he gave his notice. He always did so in ways that kept the owners from being angry, and in this case, he helped the dairy get another milker.

We didn't know it then, but our family would be destined to return to Taylorsville one more time, and my youngest sister, Helen, would be born in nearby Quincy, the closest hospital. Many years later, in 1998, I went back to Quincy and to my surprise found the century-old hospital building still standing, an amazingly small, red-brick Victorian now used as a hospital supply store.

IN 1977, I returned to Taylorsville with my three sons for a visit. The one-room school was still there, vacant and solitary in the early sunlight. Tin-roofed and red-bricked, it squatted in the yellow grass like an abandoned fort, and only closer inspection revealed how time and weather had treated it. Planks in its front were shattered, and vandals—undreamed of when I went there—had smashed a hole in the century-old bricks.

Such criminal activities by kids would have stunned the simple citizens of Taylorsville in 1939 and caused Mrs. Eldred to set her jaw even more firmly. Perhaps our simple, hands-on world spared us things like school shootings, stabbings, and drive-bys. There was nothing of value inside, unless you could count dust, memories, and the ghostly chants of children from many years ago:

> One bright morning in the middle of the night,
> Two dead boys got up to fight;
> Back to back they faced each other,
> Drew their swords, and shot each other.
> A deaf policeman heard the noise,
> And came and killed the two dead boys.

I had come back to the tiny Sierra town (population 225) for the first time in thirty-eight years, arriving early to roam undetected among childhood scenes. For strangely enough, although dad only

kept the family two years in Taylorsville, I started school there—
in this very one-room structure. To my amazement, even the tiny
two-room redwood cabin where mom, dad, Glenda, and I had lived
was still standing. I had only to walk across the road a hundred yards
to go to school. How could we have ever lived in so small a space?

I looked at the little plank cabin, red as a fox's pelt, now used as
a place to store tools and implements. Over the years, someone had
added a small lean-to. Streaked by age, it stood a hundred feet from
a small slough made by leakage from the millrace that flowed, crisp
and clear, nearby. The old grist mill is gone, but the millrace runs
on. As a child, I used to hide among the cattails that fringed the
slough, but I saw no cattails now. I wrote a poem about it in 1965
that appeared in *Harper's* magazine and several anthologies.

The Dreamer

He spent his childhood hours in a den
Of rushes, watching the grey rain braille
The surface of the river. Concealed
From the outside world, nestled within,
He was safe from parents, God, and eyes
That looked upon him accusingly,
As though to say: Even at your age,
You could do better. His camouflage
Was scant but it served, and at evening,
When fireflies burned holes into heaven,
He took the path homeward in the dark,
A small Noah, leaving his safe ark.

My three young sons were still asleep in the camper, unaware
that they were in the place where their father had begun learning
his ABCs. It would be time to awaken them soon for breakfast in
the local Grizzly Bite Café.

The tiny village had changed little. This was hunting and fishing country, and it didn't need to change. On Main Street, the
buildings were more weathered, and a few had been refaced. The
oldest one, erected a century earlier, still stood, and there was a new

store appropriately called The New Store. It was next door to Young's General Store, which I would find was now owned and operated by the tall, frosty-haired daughter of Amy Hardgrave, whose late husband owned Hardgrave's Dairy. Amy had been the one who hired my dad as a hand-milker in 1939.

The wind shifted suddenly, and I caught a whiff of skunk. I was glad it was just a whiff—we had driven many miles in cold air the night before and gone through half a dozen car washes, all because a suicidal skunk darted from roadside bushes to take up momentary residence under my left-front wheel.

The moment I hit it, I cut loose with a very bad word, because I'd encountered polecats up close and personal before, and I knew what we were in for. There was a sudden, frantic scrambling in the back of the camper, loud gagging sounds, and then my kids yelling at the tops of their lungs.

"Wow, dad, you hit a skunk!" Chris yelled.

"Ewwww! Get us out of here!" shouted Jason.

"Awkk! Ackk! Eckk!" David retched, already an overacting thespian at age six.

I had already stopped the pickup and opened the camper shell. The three of them piled out coughing, gasping, and teary-eyed. I was in the same condition. No matter which way we moved, the odor followed us.

"No use, boys," I said, after our noses were numbed. "We don't have a choice. We can't leave the truck here, and besides, we're almost in Quincy, where your Aunt Helen was born. Another twenty miles, and we'll get a motel room there. Let's squeeze into the cab—maybe most of the smell will blow backwards."

Alas, the maneuver did little to remove, or even weaken, the paralyzing odor of a perfume that can stun grizzly bears. If you've never worn *eau de polecat*, I'm here to tell you it's not one of life's great colognes.

At a motel in the small, pretty town of Quincy, the manager welcomed us with open arms—palms outward. "Mister," he said, trying not to breathe too deeply, "you gotta get that truck outta here before all my customers leave!"

"That bad?" I said, and my heart sank when he nodded. Our noses were beyond feeling, much less smelling.

The man said sympathetically, "Maybe a motel in Taylorsville will put you up. The drive there ought to blow some of that smell away."

On the way out of town, I spotted a car wash, and we ran the truck through it several times, going heavy on the soap. But skunk scent is the snapping turtle of smells—it hangs on till it thunders. It was still escorting us when we left Quincy. At least now the boys, with their novocained noses, could catnap in the back until we reached Taylorsville.

However, by the time we got there, it was past midnight, and the kids were fast asleep in back, so I found a quiet place to park and slept in the front seat until the sun struck me in the face. I had slept that way so many times as a freelancer, I often felt like a traveling salesman. Which, come to think of it, I guess I was.

"WHERE ARE we, dad?"

The camper shell's door had opened, and a sleepy Chris poked his head out. His brothers followed his lead. Breakfast smells came from a nearby café.

"Not far from where I started school in the first grade," I said. "Taylorsville, California."

"I'm hungry," said seven-year-old Jason. "How about a whole bunch of French toast?"

"It was a little one-room school," I went on. "You'll get to see it."

"Me, too," Chris said, rubbing the bottomless pit he called a stomach. Only six-year-old David, soon to start kindergarten, had perked up at the mention of the word *school*. Maybe if I ducked the other two in nearby Indian Creek, which trundled like a silver brook through the town, they'd show more interest in their old man's childhood.

Oh, well. *Don't tell us what you've done, tell us what you're going to do—for us.* I herded them into the café, where a bunch of French toast wasn't available, and they had to settle for pancakes. After breakfast, my kids found a mob of other kids, and soon they were swarming around the Grizzly Bite Café, killing each other with loaded fingers. It was a nice place, under huge trees, with a big log on the ground to sit on. I asked the owner, a motherly lady, if I could leave the boys there for awhile. I'd be happy to pay, I said.

"Pshaw," she snorted. "Just leave 'em with mine out there. They'll be fine." The Grizzly Bite was heaven for my kids. They not only had others to play with, they could also gobble the place's specialty, homemade bear claws shaped like a grizzly bear's paw.

Taylorsville is a tiny, beautiful town, lush and green in the spring and summer, and in the fall, surrounded by trees with leaves like gold coins. Reposing in gorgeous Indian Valley at seven thousand feet, it's laced by clear, shining brooks. Just to the north are the headwaters of the Feather River, cutting a swath through some of Northern California's most majestic mountains. It's prime hunting and fishing country, and even when I was a kid there in 1939, tourism was brisk. It was common, during the season, to see some hunter chugging down out of the hills with a deer or black bear tied to his front fender. Pines and firs stud the mountains' flanks like green feathers—a beauty that carries over into winter, which, at seven thousand plus feet, can be brutal.

IN SEPTEMBER 1939, with mom's abdomen now fully distended, we returned to Phoenix where we would spend the winter with dad's brother Bid and his wife, Sam. They had come back from Oklahoma for jobs in Phoenix. Then as now, people followed the jobs. Uncle Bid and Aunt Sam were in and out of our lives several times over the years. I liked Bid because he always quoted folksy riddles or axioms to me like this:

> A wise old owl sat in an oak
> The more he heard the less he spoke

> The less he spoke the more he heard
> Why can't women imitate that bird?

But my favorite was:

> Brothers and sisters
> Have I none,
> But that man's father
> Is my father's son.

Maybe the reason I liked it so much was that I never could figure it out. At first, I thought it was a boy staring in a mirror, but that didn't seem right, and Uncle Bid refused to tell me the answer—if he even knew.

In mid-October, my brother David was born, an infant of less than five pounds. He was a blue baby and for weeks remained in the hospital in an oxygen tent, hovering between life and death. Mom smoked heavily during pregnancy—everyone smoked then—and that may have caused problems for my brother. But no one knew anything about the poisonous nature of tobacco in those days, and such afflictions were sometimes fatal to infants. Indeed, mom and dad were called late one night and told that if they wanted to see their baby alive, they had to come at once. Mom told the story many times, usually quite dramatically. She could sing beautifully and also tell a gripping story, doing both in the hillbilly way, with long, melodramatic word extensions like, "Oh-h-h-h, Lor-r-r-rd, if you could've se-e-e-en that pore baby!" (Today, David is a contractor who tips the scales at roughly two hundred and fifty pounds, or fifty times what he weighed in the oxygen tent.)

Dad eventually found us a house of our own and brought my brother home from the hospital, where he slowly grew healthy. Dad then went to work in a flour mill in nearby Glendale, and sometimes mom would drive down at lunchtime, with my baby brother wrapped on the seat beside her and with me proudly holding him so he wouldn't fall.

UNTIL I ESCAPED into the army in 1951, my father shuttled the family back and forth from east to west so frequently, we probably wore a trail. We moved so much and so often, the only way I can give you the substance of it is to dish up events I can remember. Suffice to say, from 1938 to 1952, our family averaged moving once a year from the Ozarks to California and most points between.

It didn't take dad long to teach me about work. He started me picking cotton at age six with a burlap sack strapped to my skinny frame. In a week, I might pick fifty pounds, which, at the going wage of fifty cents per hundred, meant I earned two bits—or one twenty-fourth of an adult's wage. Dad kept it, of course, although he sometimes parted with a nickel for Sunday school if I worked extra hard. I saw no point in giving my hard-earned nickel to some preacher I couldn't even understand, and I didn't like Sunday school anyway, so I usually spent it on a snow cone.

I was enrolled in many schools over those years and taken out many times to harvest our meager crops, or go on the road, or move to another state, or head back west. Sometimes, though, dad had a real job, especially during World War II when he took a job as a copper miner in Miami, Arizona. Occasionally, he followed the wheat harvest in Colorado and Montana, driving trucks filled with grain to elevators, and it could be six weeks before he came back home. During that time, mom and I kept the farm going, slopping the pigs, milking the cows, and preparing for winter.

We picked cotton around Firebaugh, California, several times over the years. Dad not only hired out the family as cotton pickers, but he and mom also tried to establish a secondhand store there. It soon folded. Neither of them were business people, although mom was better than dad when it came to money.

Firebaugh was a shabby little hamlet in 1940, surrounded by vast fields of cotton and scattered pickers' shacks. We occupied an actual house—dilapidated, but better than a shack. One night, my parents got in a row, and mom grabbed a brass alarm clock, wound up like Joe DiMaggio, and winged it at dad. The clock, which must have weighed a pound, bounced off his head and knocked him flat.

Blood flowed, and mom, startled by her achievement, began swabbing the cut with a towel.

"Dang it, hon," she crooned. "You always ducked before."

It was too late to make peace. The cops came, and my folks spent the night in jail. The next day, much subdued, they came home with bedbug bites all over them. It wasn't the first time they fought, and it wouldn't be the last. Both dad and mom had tempers. Mom's red hair signaled the Irish in her, and she could go off like a hand grenade. They had more than a few melees, for those were rough times, and the strains of poverty made tempers flare. Mom wasn't small, either. She grew up working alongside men, and took no guff from anyone.

Dad's biggest weakness wasn't liquor or women, it was cars. At any given time, we might hear a horn blow and look out to see a strange car in the driveway, and behind the wheel would be dad, grinning like a teenager with a new girlfriend. One time mom got so furious at this waste of money that she ran out and twisted the mirror off dad's latest toy—a Dodge pickup—with her bare hands. Then she and dad went round and round. Boy, was she mad. We kids looked through the window and were glad to be inside. But if he lived through the first round, dad had an uncanny gift for cooling her down, and such was the case here. He ended up keeping the pickup but had to have the mirror fixed. Dad bought at least one car for every year of his life—most of them used, but in later years, some new ones.

As a kid, I naturally found it fascinating that my folks were jailbirds—if only for a night. I knew that in my budding dream of being a writer, there would be a place for such adventures. It gave them a certain status, I thought. It set them apart from our humdrum law-abiding neighbors. Sometimes I fantasized that my parents were the reincarnation of Bonnie and Clyde. But there was the problem of the banks robbing them instead of vice versa. Dad tried buying a farm once but soon lost it back to the bank. For some time after that, he kept all his money in the back of a cupboard.

If I had mentioned their fracases while dad was alive, he might have come up beside my head with a singletree—and if he didn't, mom would have. I thought such secrecy was foolish. To begin with, it wasn't even a secret. Everyone in the family, as well as anyone living near us, knew about their fights. But I respected their wishes and waited until they (and many others in this book) were dead.

THE GREAT DEPRESSION didn't really end until after Pearl Harbor, which pushed us into the war that was already engulfing the rest of the world. Before this, dad worked at any job that put food on the table. In late 1942, we again found ourselves in Arizona. I was nine, Glenda was four, David three, and Helen not yet a year old. My siblings were too young to understand the situation, but I wasn't. I saw in dad's face the glum despair of going for a job interview and being refused for one reason or other—often because someone just got there first. Then as now, folks followed the employment highway, and rumors of hiring in some other town would take them there. So it was that dad heard about a big start-up in copper production for the war looming in all our minds and took the family to a little town east of Phoenix called Miami.

Miami's companion towns were Globe, Claypool, and Central Heights, all of them dusty, high-desert towns of white tailings and bleak, rocky hills. Cactus dotted the arid earth, and the towns perched precariously on the sides of cliffs with narrow white roads snaking up to tin-roofed houses. Miami was a depressingly ugly place, but one of dad's brothers, Ray, lived and worked there as a copper miner all his life. He's buried in a solitary grave outside of Miami. Today, of course, Miami is a larger, more modern town. But very little copper has been mined there since World War II, and the Miami Copper Company that hired dad a month before Christmas has long since closed the mine.

Years later, when I asked dad about his Arizona memories, he told me that going to copper country hadn't produced any miracles. Many a morning I remember being awakened by his rummaging around in the cold desert darkness, preparing to drive fifty miles before dawn to a spot on the highway where he sold fruit from the back of a truck. He would park the battered old pickup, loaded with melons, oranges, and other fruit, where travelers were plentiful and where there was space for them to pull over, which was a gas station and garage called Apache Junction. Today it's a town of about twenty-five thousand people. This went on for weeks, as he took whatever jobs he could get while we lived with the family of his brother Ray, who already had a job in the mine.

In the crowded company house, Ray's wife and my mother barely tolerated each other, and the two men walked on eggshells trying to keep things peaceful. Aunt Una was beautiful and sexy, with the smile of a gypsy tease. Mom, always insecure around such women, was torn by jealousy. Not only did they never get to be friends, more than once they engaged in hair-pulling combat. Before they could murder each other, dad found regular work, and we rented our own house.

Uncle Ray was older than dad and was in my life a couple of times, the longest being that time when dad worked in the mines during the war. Ray's kids were Ray Jr. (whom we all called "Junior"), Lela, and Martha, and we played together as kids in the chalk-white dust of the tailings—hide-and-seek, kick-the-can, and cowboys-and-Indians. I loved my cousins, and we had a lot of fun when we weren't affected by some family problem or other.

At its wartime peak, the Miami Copper Company would employ three thousand miners at starting wages of $5 a day. No benefits, no vacation, no hospitalization, no union—and no complaints. "We was damned glad to get it," dad later said. "We'd been makin' a lot less." The war was gearing up, and changes were coming thick and fast. For the first time in his life, dad had credit, and he opened a charge account with the Sears, Roebuck mail-order house. "I had a steady job and no debts. That made me a good credit risk, I guess. Anyway, we was able to give you kids the best Christmas you'd ever had."

Dad would do fine at such jobs for awhile, but then his feet would itch, and homesickness would drift over him like a dust-bowl cloud. "Wild horses couldn't keep him from Oklahoma when he was like that," mom once said. I guess we shouldn't have been surprised. Oklahoma was where dad was born and grew up, and even though a life of roving took him many places, he always came back to Oklahoma. He died there eventually but chose to be buried in Missouri, a mile from his farm.

Dad worked in the copper mines then for almost two years but was destined to return to Miami one more time when we kids were older, mom more eccentric, and the family just as destitute as ever. I attended third grade in Miami in 1943, and after bits and pieces of schooling elsewhere, graduated from the eighth grade there five years later.

Dad sometimes brought lunch buckets full of turquoise up from underground, and if I had those blue rocks now, I'd be wealthy. But they weren't nearly as precious then as they are today. Dad would sell them to a local jeweler for a buck or two.

But once the war began winding down, his feet began itching again, and he had a little money saved. What better use for it than another farm? So he quit, bought a used brown 1939 Hudson, and once more we headed down the highway, pulling a trailer loaded with our stuff, covered with a tarp, and tied down.

Road-toads again.

We worked our way back to Oklahoma, where dad leased another exhausted farm "on the shares." It was the middle of 1944. Years later, I discovered that he had a more important reason to head for Oklahoma. He was afraid he would be drafted—even though his four children made him 4-F. He'd been in the army briefly in the early 1930s but hated it so much he bought his way out and wasn't about to go back in. Farmers, you see, were exempt from the draft.

IN 1994, I found myself once again in Miami, Arizona. Half a century later, almost a lifetime, a freelance trip had taken me there during a westward swing with my twenty-two-year-old son David. I had gotten a phone number from dad before leaving, and in the little mining town of Globe, I telephoned Martha, Ray's youngest daughter, a high school counselor in the Globe school system. At first, she didn't believe it was me, but I finally persuaded her that it was, and she promised to meet us as soon as she could. She said her brother, Junior, was retired and lived elsewhere, and that her sister, Lela Mae, had been struck and killed by a car when she ran across a California freeway. There was more to the story, which I will relate to you later.

Not far from the service station where we were parked lay a copper kingdom. How could I explain those long-ago days to my son? The badges of its industry now lay bleached by the sun—white, steep-sided tailings, a mountain of black slag, jumbled tanks, and buildings clumped on hillsides. High on a hill stood a rusty steel elevator tower. It was connected to a shaft that once dropped miners hundreds of feet into utter darkness, to where arcs of wavering bulbs writhed through the tunnels like golden serpents. Dad and Ray descended every night into that gloom to dig the copper for World War II.

Under a sky so hot it was whitish-blue, the huge cable wheel posed like a sea serpent caught in mid-arc. The buildings were rusted and dead. They had not known the tread of people for decades, and the entire complex was surrounded by a cyclone fence—itself old and rusted. Fascinated by the giant equipment, my son peered up at the one-hundred-foot tower.

"How big do you think that wheel is on top, dad?" he asked.

"Sixteen feet in diameter," I said, for that was what dad had told me when I mentioned that I was going back to write a story about the copper town where he once worked.

"Wow," David said. "That's big."

A new car appeared beside mine with a smiling woman behind the wheel. David and I got out to shake hands with Martha, slim and elegant in a new suit. She had her mother's face and her father's eyes. She had never seen David, or any of my other kids, and she hugged him.

"I wasn't sure it was you," she said. "Now that I see it is, I'm so excited I can hardly stand it!"

"Me too," I said. "You look a lot like your mom, Una."

An expression flitted across her face that I couldn't interpret, and she said, "How's J. W.?"

"Dad's doing okay," I said. "But we lost mom two years ago to brain cancer."

Martha looked stricken for a moment but then regained control. "It's been so long since I saw any of you," she said sadly, "that I can barely remember what Lorraine looked like."

"Well, she kept her famous temper almost to the end."

"Oh, my gosh!"

"Remember the time she and your mom mixed it up?" I said. "Enough red and black hair was pulled that day to stuff a sofa."

"My mom and yours," Martha, whose own hair was blond, chuckled. "I never saw two women who were less afraid of physical combat than they were."

David, who is gradually becoming the custodian of family legends, stood off to one side, quietly listening. A slight breeze sprang up, hot as flame, pushing dead weeds across the asphalt.

"Well," Martha said, "let's go home, and I'll fix you guys something to eat."

GLOBE HAD CHANGED. I remembered it as a dusty little nothing of a town where I had briefly gone to second grade. I remembered the teacher, too—a mean, spiteful woman named Miss Day. If I believed in voodoo, I'd still be sticking pins in her doll. Surprisingly, the café where I had last seen Martha's mother, Una, in 1949 was still in business—as it had been since 1919. This was its seventy-fifth year.

Martha is seven years younger than I, and when my cousins and I played together, she was considered a pest, like my own younger siblings. In the mindless cruelty of growing children, we didn't want little kids in our games. Usually, they ended up playing anyway.

There was something else we did as kids: we spent a lot of time trying to understand the turbulent natures of our parents. As my son and I followed Martha's car to a spacious home framed by rolling hills, I reflected that this was the first time two of our family's children had dug into the turmoil of their past. I had seen Martha only once since 1944, during a brief visit in 1959. She was a harried young mother with two small children then; her kids were now in their thirties. How very long ago it all was, and yet we could conjure up memories fresher than dew.

We became time travelers, plunging into our past as if searching for absolution or release. I'm not sure why. Maybe it was a journey we both felt obligated to attempt. Who can ever really understand their parents, or why they do the things they do—good or bad?

For Martha and me, childhood in the copper kingdom was violent at times. It was impossible for us to understand the shouting our parents engaged in. We feared the screams and blows and hid from all of it, but we never, ever understood it. Gradually, we began to understand that at least some of the violence was linked to whiskey. Our family had its share of alcoholics, including Martha's mother and mine.

"I think violent tendencies can be inherited," she said. "I think so every time I remember mom and my dead sister, Lela Mae. They were carbon copies of each other, both wanting fast times and the good life and wanting it the easy way. Mom broke dad's heart many times over, and when Lela died the way she did, it just took everything out of him." Even now, in 1994, she missed her father—dead for fifteen years. She didn't miss her mother, though. Una was cruelly abusive, drifted into prostitution, and ended her days as a broken-down alcoholic.

"The things she did to us as a family are very, very hard to forgive," Martha said. Martha was four and I was eleven when we witnessed a violent scene between Ray and Una. Junior, Lela, Martha, and I were outside playing when a drunken Ray came weaving out of the tin-roofed shack that poor people like us lived in. The rickety door banged open, and Una ran out, brandishing a stick of stove wood. Rushing up behind her husband, she smashed him over the head. Ray crumpled like a sack of laundry, and I remember his son and daughters running up to his fallen form, crying and trying to revive him. Their mother, in behavior that was to become her trademark, coldly turned and stalked back into the house, a young and beautiful woman with a murderous temper.

As kids in the copper towns in World War II, we played with the sense of abandon young children enjoy. Play was our panacea. Even our dysfunctional parents and their frequent battles could be pushed out of our minds by a good game of kick-the-can. It may have been that ability that helped Martha and me survive with less severe problems—the only two of seven kids who did. For the kids we were in 1943 never died; they're still inside of us, and in each of us at different times, the fear came back and overwhelmed us and made us sick. Yes, we hid it well. We went on and lived lifetimes in spite of it, but the lifetimes were—one way or another—always flawed.

When Martha grew up and married, she had three children. Her older sister Lela also had three. But the two sisters never got along or had much to do with each other. "Lela patterned herself after mom," Martha said. "She wanted fancy clothes, and she knew sex was the way to get anything she wanted. She was beautiful, and she knew it. She married three times before she died at thirty-five."

Martha's voice was low as she recalled her beautiful blond sister and the furious, almost desperate, life she had lived. Lela, the poor kid from tin-roofed-shack towns, hemmed in by the white tailings of copper mines, had never wanted anything more than love and understanding. But the only way she knew how to get them had already been proven false by her mother.

"It wouldn't have been so bad if it was only her," Martha said. "But there were the children, too. For Lela, though, only Lela mattered. She imitated mom much too well." Years and husbands passed, and Lela Mae drifted farther away from her family. Her own mother, sunk in alcohol, was hateful and resentful. Una had finally ended her tormented marriage to Ray and married a fellow alcoholic. Remarkably, they stayed together until he died of cirrhosis.

Somewhere in the web of time, Lela had contacted her younger sister. "She seemed to want to make amends," Martha recalled. "She breezed into town in a red convertible, dressed to the nines, but she was no longer the sister I once knew. After all, it had been seventeen years since I had last seen her." The visit was hard for both sisters, and when Lela finally walked to her car to leave, she gave

Martha a hug and said, "I know I haven't always been a good sister to you, but I have always loved you." It would be the last thing Martha heard from her. Then one night her father, in a voice full of pain, called to say, "Lela Mae has been killed in Calexico. I'm going down there."

When Lela was killed on a California highway, she had been partying far from her kids, leaving them alone in a motel while she went out to have a good time. She had left her eleven-year-old son in charge of the smaller children. But she wasn't beautiful when they took her to the hospital. Her legs were broken and her skull fractured from cars running over her on the pavement. She lingered for a few hours before she died. So often had their mother left them alone, the kids didn't even know she was dead for several hours, until the police came and took the eleven-year-old boy outside and told him. Then they went inside with him and told the younger kids.

"People who saw her that night say she left the bar and ran across the freeway," Martha remembered. "Then she turned and started to run back, and that was when she was hit. They said she seemed confused, but I think she was just tired of her life. The booze and the parties no longer filled the void of her childhood. She never had any acceptance as a child, and all her life, she wanted acceptance more than anything. She acquired material things, thinking it would make people see her as a success. She left three kids and a sports car as her legacy."

Martha drove with her father down to Calexico, not quite a day's drive from Miami, and together they went to see Lela's children. "The place was strewn with garbage," Martha said. "But the kids did have money. Lela always left them money when she went off on her wild parties. It was obvious she had done this many times before."

Lela Mae, the cousin I played hide-and-seek and kick-the-can with, is buried in Calexico. Someday, if I live long enough, I want to visit her grave. The last anyone knew of the kids, they were taken by their father. He had long since divorced Lela—to whom the judge inexplicably gave custody of the children. Today, they're grown and pursuing lives of their own.

After the death of his oldest daughter, Uncle Ray went into slow decline. In 1980, Raymond Hugh Childress, who was ten years old when a heart attack killed his own father, died of a ruptured aorta. He was sixty-eight. He's buried in a lone grave by a highway near Miami.

Una, lost in the fumes of alcohol, had long since lost interest in the family. In her old age, she became an increasing burden for her overworked daughter. Martha was finally forced to place her mother, almost dead from alcohol poisoning, into a nursing home. Used to getting her way, Una begged and cajoled Martha not to do it, but Martha had tried keeping her at home, and it proved impossible.

"You were just killing yourself with alcohol," Martha told her mother. She said that Una's eyes turned cold and hateful.

"Then get the goddamn hell out of here," Una rasped. "You're not my daughter anymore."

For the final six years of her life, Una refused to see the daughter who had done so much for her and whose own life she had so mutilated. When she finally lay dying, the nursing home called Martha, who went down one final time to see if she could help.

"I heard her hoarse breathing as I walked down the hallway," Martha said. "The doctor suspected cancer because mom was a heavy smoker as well as drinker. But she refused exploratory surgery. She was choking for air when I walked in, a terrible sound to hear. But when I went to her bedside and said, 'Mom, do you want me to stay?' her eyes took on the hardest look of rage I'd ever seen. She couldn't speak, but she used her last strength to wave me violently out of the room. I heard her breathing stop as I walked down the corridor." Una is buried near Safford, Arizona, but nobody ever visits her grave.

Martha told me much of this while driving David and me to some of the old places where our parents had lived—and fought—and where we played as children. Amazingly, many of them still stood, and I stopped to talk with a Mexican family who now lived in the same old tin-roofed house I had occupied forty-seven years earlier.

"Aqui es mi casa en 1947," I said in my copper-town Spanish. They stared at me, a gringo geezer they'd never laid eyes on, probably

thinking I was *loco*, or at best thinking my Spanish was impossible to understand.

I HAVE OTHER MEMORIES of those years in Arizona that are as vivid today as if they happened yesterday. There was a store in Central Heights, not far from Miami, whose owner was a lay minister, the only female preacher I'd ever seen in my young life. She was a hand-wiggling, shouting woman, and one of the worst scares I ever had was when mom took me to the vacant building the old biddy called her church. I was the only kid, and there were just a few women in the room.

The preacher started hollering for the Lord to come down and cast the devils out of this darling child, said darling child being held down by his mother and four other women while he frantically tried to escape. The harder I strove, the more that old bat caterwauled that Satan had his hooks in me, sure enough, and for the ladies to hold on, now, and not be whipped by no devil. What saved me was that I simply gave up and slumped, squalling. All of them (including mom) took that as a sure sign that the devil had left me, and the building fairly shook with hallelujahs. For a long time after that, I went around wondering how God put up with such people.

Then there was the Hill Street School, where I had gone to second grade. When I visited in 1994, it still stood in Globe—but it had been empty for years. And Miami Elementary had been torn down. I got swats from Miami Elem's principal, Mr. Case, who would be about a hundred and ten years old now. I also got swats from Mrs. Dunsmore, who was built like a football player and looked like one. When she swung the paddle, it lifted me clear off the floor. But it taught me never to eat peanuts in her class.

Going back into the past is a journey everyone should take at least once. But sometimes in the process of reviewing our lives, my eyes fill with tears. I turn away to hide them, but I don't think I'm always successful.

2

FROM THE TORNADOES of his boyhood to the terrible dust storms of the 1930s, my dad knew about winds. He grew up in plains country where winds wailed like banshees during spring storms, clouds turned licorice black, and cyclone cells could form in an instant. He must have missed all that excitement, because after he got married and started a family in nice, warm Arizona, he hauled us back to Oklahoma, where winter winds howled across the plains like invisible wolves. My ears and toes are still stinging.

But like willow trees, kids bend to the winds of change. Not much fazed us. In fact, each move was a new adventure. We didn't even care if some of them were bad ones—we didn't have to walk for gas when the car ran dry. When we drove into any new place, we always found beautiful things or sources of fun, because what we cared most about sat up front—sometimes quarreling, sometimes peaceful, but always our parents and always our security. Although we never thought of it quite that way, because of them we had food and shelter. In the main, though, the places where we kids ended up suited us fine, no matter how shabby.

And shabby is what they were. Gray, old, 1920s farmhouses, never taken care of, often with their tin roofs half peeled away. Floors warped and splintery, sagging porches, broken windows. Rusty pumps in the yard with leather gaskets so dry they wouldn't pump water—assuming the well had any. If the place had a cistern, we kids watched fascinated as dad fished out dead rats and birds and then gurgled a gallon of bleach into it that would kill the germs and give the water an awful flavor. Mom would also make a point of boiling it.

My father was to carpentry what I am to brain surgery, but he fixed what he could. Such shacks were never homes; they were huts with blankets hiding broken windows, a tin stove for cooking and heating, and no trees or flowers. The yards were forests of weeds, which meant a call went out for me and my hoe. In winter, we stuffed rags and newspapers in wall cracks to keep the wind out, but it didn't help much.

Shortly before we found the Pokero place in 1944, dad rented a real rattrap in Indiahoma—undoubtedly because it was so cheap— and since I barely weighed sixty pounds, he sent me up to check on the roof. I hollered down and told him the roof was in bad shape, which didn't fill him with joy. "Well, hell," he yelled up at me, "crawl out there on that lean-to porch and check it, then." The lean-to was used as a better-than-nothing laundry room.

"Okay," I answered. Never well made, the lean-to wobbled under me, and I started to have doubts about going on, when the decision was taken from me. The spot I stood on disintegrated, and down I went in a cloud of dusty shingles onto a pile of laundry that mom was washing. She looked at me, her sudsy hands still poised over a washboard and galvanized tub. All she did was look at me, I guess in shock.

I was dusting myself off when dad stuck his head in the door, saw me standing, and started to leave. To say the least, that did not please mom.

"Ain't you even going to see if he's *hurt?*" she shouted.

"Hell's bells, anybody can *see* he ain't hurt!" dad roared, probably feeling sorry for himself for having rented the dump. But his reply ignited mom's dynamite temper, and she exploded.

"You selfish bastard! If it was you, you'd be hollerin' to high heaven. I can't stand you!"

"Awww, the hell you whistle!" dad said and stomped off. Great! Now I had him mad at me and both of them mad at each other. If the old man got mad enough (and mom knew how to inspire it), he wasn't averse to treating me like crap for the rest of the day.

That was the pattern my younger siblings and I would see and hear, over and over, through our growing years. We ignored as much as we could but were always tense and on edge when our parents acted up, fearing the more violent explosions that our experience told us were sure to come, knowing that eventually they would spill over onto us.

WE LEFT INDIAHOMA as soon as we could and settled on a farm east of Lawton and north of Pumpkin Center. I remember this land as bleak and flat, with very low rolling hills and scrub trees, except for larger pecan trees along Big Beaver Creek. The pastures in March were ragged and yellow, and the trees skeletal. Fences staggered off across fields like derelict drunks, their posts weakened by age. A heavily rutted red-clay road led to the farm. A real loblolly when it rained, the road trapped many a car in its thick gumbo mud. It was such ugly country, not even my overactive imagination could make it pretty. I often wondered what mom thought of some of these places, but I guess she was too busy scrubbing them clean with bleach and Lysol to see how dismal they were.

In 1944, Charlie Pokero, a heavy-set Choctaw Indian, owned the farm, and since it came with a house (if you could call it that), dad contracted to farm it on the shares. He would plant cotton, oats, and corn—the corn being for the hogs he hadn't bought yet. The place had a rusty pump in the yard, a chicken house, a beat-up barn, an abandoned granary, and cow corrals made of sheep wire. Behind the barn, a creaky windmill splashed a slow stream of water into a concrete stock tank.

None of us could imagine it then, but dad would actually make this place fairly successful. I doubt even he knew how he did it, but by the time we sold out at war's end, we had fourteen horses, a tractor and equipment, twenty-eight milking cows, and twenty-five head of hogs. Alas, the bottom had fallen out of the livestock market at the time we sold, and we left the experiment with little to show for two years of hard labor. Dad's inept management style would give mom fuel for future fires.

The first year, though, dad planted his crops in the spring and bought pigs and other livestock, and the weather being good, with rains coming just right, the cotton, corn, and maize grew thick and green. I loved the rows when the crops were just beginning, little emerald spears straight as string, until by late spring the fields were rippling blankets of jade. Good time to become a turkey herder.

MY OLD MAN had more secrets than Los Alamos, so I never had an inkling of why he got into the turkey business. I think his reasoning may have gone like this: (1) More turkeys are needed to feed a growing population. (2) I have a kid who can herd them.

Turkeys today live in fancy pens and houses and are produced in huge numbers, but when I was a kid, the business was still new enough for small farmers to "free range" their modest flocks of gobblers. So . . .

"I'm gonna buy some turkeys," dad announced one day.

"Turkeys?" mom said. "Why?"

"Lotsa grasshoppers this year," dad went on, "and the birds can take advantage of the green grass. Besides, it'll give Bill something to do." He didn't actually say those last seven words, but I knew he was thinking them. For darn sure, *he* wasn't going to herd any turkeys.

Now, in case you haven't heard, the epitome of stupidity is neither cows nor sheep, although both rank way down there. It's *Meleagris gallopavo*, the common American turkey. I'm an admirer of Benjamin Franklin, but when he suggested the turkey over the eagle as our national bird, he had to be suffering from electric shock. Ben was a joker, though, and might have been kidding.

Perhaps some folk wisdom will put the matter in perspective. It's been said that if a man touched a hot stove, he wouldn't touch a *cold* stove after that. A turkey, on the other hand, would go back to the hot stove and try to hatch her chicks there.

In due time I found myself, long willow switch in hand, herding a flock of fifty gobbling birds along the creek bank and through dad's fields. I soon found that this was a lot like trying to control a bunch of flightless storks. Turkeys only run when they see a grasshopper, and then they're faster than a speeding pullet. The other turkeys see that one running, and all take off after him, just in case there's enough grasshopper to feed fifty. A mighty battle ensues, with much gobbling and wing flapping. Usually, the first one to spot the bug gets it, but I have seen upwards of six half-grown birds pecking at the victor, trying to make him drop even so much as a wing membrane.

Eventually, by calling "Klook, klook, klook, klook!" and waving the small rag tied to the willow wand, I got them back into a semblance of order. I felt like the biggest dope in the world as those gobbling pea-brains ambled along eating grass, worms, scurrying insects, or the ever-present grasshoppers.

"Why do I have to herd those dang turkeys?" I griped after the first day.

"Because if you don't," dad said, "they'll be over in the next county in no time at all."

"They can't even fly, for cat's sake!"

"No, but they can run. Now shut up about it."

The turkeys grew fast, and in due time, they were ready for market. Dad's luck held true. He'd bought them when the hatch price was low and the market price was high. But after spending money to grow them, even with free labor, he found that the market had shriveled. He barely broke even and never messed with *Meleagris gallopavo* again.

LIKE WIND BLOWING past a cave, the plane's engines fill the cabin with hollow sound. The trip from Sacramento has been uneventful, and most of the passengers in the half-full plane are dozing. I wondered how many were on similar journeys or had melancholy events of their own to contend with. I had tried to read the glossy collection of ads the airline called a magazine, but the storm in my mind saved me. As if on a screen inside it, I kept seeing events from our lives.

The airline lunch was a bun, a skimpy meat patty, lettuce, pickle, and two spoon-sized pieces of watermelon so thin you could read through them. Even at times like this, or perhaps because of them, the tiny semicircles reminded me of my favorite occupation when I was growing up. No sooner had dad taken us to his first Oklahoma farm (the old, exhausted Pokero place near Lawton) than I became aware of that kingly fruit called watermelon. All the farmers raised at least a patch, and I wondered about the name. It tasted so much better than water, my ten-year-old mind considered a few replacements. Why not *ambrosia melon* or *nectar melon*?

But we were in Oklahoma, and creative thinking was neither admired nor rewarded. Where I grew up, *thinking* came wrapped in a Bible. Oklahoma cursed Woody Guthrie as a communist, drove poet John Berryman to suicide, and treated black author Ralph Ellison like dirt. But, to its credit, it did give Will Rogers to the world.

Dad was addicted to red dirt, a fundamentalist existence, and impossible poverty, all of which Oklahoma had plenty of. Not that he was religious. To paraphrase poet T. S. Eliot, dad just wasn't one to kick against the pricks. Continuing what would be a ten-year trend in his life, he leased a farm near Rush Springs, the self-styled "Watermelon Capital of the World." He and his brother Tom hoped to raise the melons as a cash crop, but light, sandy soil is best for that, and the clay gumbo on dad's lease was no good. The same was true of Tom's farm, two miles down the road, which had the same kind of dirt. We kids were mystified that our fathers knew so little about farming but practiced it so much.

"THERE AIN'T a thing left to do but steal 'em," declared Tom's sons, my cousins Jimmy and Johnny. Having no willpower of my own at age eleven, I agreed—and as a result of several crime sprees in that direction, my conscience has hurt me ever since. However, those early forays made me sure I'd found my life's profession. A small but strong body made me one of the best watermelon rustlers around, and I saw no reason why I couldn't keep it up until the arthritis got too bad. Besides, I'd earned the badges such a career merits—rock salt dimples on my rump.

Jimmy and Johnny were my companions in crime for years, but we never took more than we could eat. However, sharecrop kids are often hungry, and we ate a lot. One time we were so famished, watermelon wouldn't satisfy us. So we decided to branch out, steal a chicken, and cook it down by the creek. But where to find a chicken?

"The Dutchman!" Johnny said excitedly. "He's got so many, he ain't gonna miss one!"

So one night, when the wind blew from the dogs to us, we lit out for the Dutchman's farm and cut a hole in his chicken wire. As the smallest, it was my job to squirm through and bring out a hen. Or a rooster. We weren't particular. The only trouble was, I had barely got inside when the wind shifted. The dogs caught Jimmy's and Johnny's scent, promptly went crazy, and my cowardly cousins took off like rockets, with the dogs yapping furiously in their wake. The dogs hadn't caught my scent because I was already in the hen house, under thirty dozing hens and a couple of roosters perched on transverse limbs nailed up as roosts. The Dutchman, whose English was hopeless, was a skinflint who didn't waste money on good lumber.

Suddenly a screen door slammed, and a voice chided the dogs fondly, saying, "Hah, ya got dem goddamn chicken t'ieves, yah? Vell, ve go see, den! But I tink I saw you chasin' dem 'cross da feel, yah?"

Aside from deciphering "got dem" from "goddamn," I realized my chicken-thieving goose was cooked and wondered if I should just crawl out, blubbering, and throw myself on the mercy of the Dutchman. This avenue was becoming more tempting because several chickens had developed loose bowels and were sharing them with me.

The god of chicken thieves must have been with me that night, because the old man never found the hole. He barely glanced into the dim chicken house. As for the dogs, they smelled only *eau de pullet*, and I was spared. I crawled out when he took the hounds back in the house to feed them and skedaddled across the field, mad as hell at my cousins—especially when I saw the state of my only unpatched shirt.

"Mama's gonna wonder how I got chicken doo-doo on this shirt!" I yelled at them.

"What could we do?" Johnny argued. "We'd've been up crap creek if we'd've got caught—which means you'd've been caught, too."

Watermelon heists, though not without risk, were safer than pilfering chickens, so we returned to our former careers. Filching this divine fruit, even if a sheriff's deputy tells you otherwise, is a childhood rite of passage, almost religious in its significance. If a boy returned uncaught from his first raid, it was a minor triumph. If he came back grinning with his face wet and his overall bib slick from juice, it was a major triumph. He was promoted yet another step if he brought a melon back with him, and if a shotgun went off during any of this, he was likely to be canonized. The only thing higher was to get peppered with rock salt, which hurt like hell but didn't last long. Most farmers simply shot into the air and roared with laughter as two or three urchins erupted from the vines and scampered for the fence.

Some farmers, though, were grouch-guts devoid of mirth and lacking in charity. They saw nothing funny in some of their finest melons disappearing overnight, not to mention two or three more being busted open for the delicious, seedless heart meat. But the gains outweighed the risks, so when summer hit full stride, Jimmy and Johnny came hotfooting through the cow pasture hollering, "Watermelon time!"

Soon we were down at the creek, diving off a fallen log into the latest swimming hole left by spring rains and making plans.

"Who do we steal from this year?" I asked Jimmy.

"Ol' man Jessup," Jimmy answered. "He's got fifty acres, and he shore won't miss a few."

"Ol' man Jessup has a shotgun," Johnny pointed out.

"And dogs," I added.

"Aw, for cat's sake!" Jimmy said, spitting scornfully through a gap in his front teeth. Johnny and I envied that feat. We'd seen him drown a tumblebug six feet away in tobacco juice.

"Them hounds of his won't bite nothin' but a biscuit," Jimmy went on. "And ol' man Jessup couldn't hit a bull in the ass with a bale of hay. You guys turnin' chicken?" We vigorously denied that awful possibility and raided old man Jessup's melon patch that very night. But somehow our commando tactics came a cropper, and his dogs chased us through a field of nettles for our pains.

BELIEVE ME when I tell you that the best judge of a watermelon is a kid. Grown-ups poke and thump and look wise, but kids don't mess around. They have style. The riper and sweeter a melon is, the deeper kids will snorkel into it, to emerge belching and grinning and as sticky as if they had worked all day in a sorghum factory. Grown-ups simply can't match dedication like that.

Dad and some of his chums once developed a system for starting creekside patches. They'd roll half a dozen melons into the water, where they floated, and the boys would swim down the creek, pushing them along. Under the right conditions, watermelons can reach amazing sizes. One reached 262 pounds in Tennessee in 1990, and I heard of one that weighed 1,000 pounds but couldn't track it down. At that size, though, the innards are bound to be more mush than melon.

Once, while picking cotton in a muddy bottom, I stumbled over the biggest watermelon I'd ever seen. It was hidden in a welter of vines and cotton stalks and had probably lain there since a politician last told the truth. With a shout of excitement, I shucked my sack and raced back down the rows to tell my folks. Dad came, and after a few grunts, got the monster in his arms and lugged it to the scales—where it weighed 83 pounds on the cotton scales. Dad invited several other pickers to help eat it.

I rubbed my hands. What a feast we were about to have! With a flourish, dad stabbed his Case knife into the huge oval. It split with a sound like paper tearing, and oh, the jewel-red interior gleaming with juices and rich as velvet that met our eyes! A thousand sugary diamonds reflected the sunlight—and right there I should've gotten suspicious. The answer came a moment later, when dad ceremoniously cut and handed a chunk to mom.

"Yum," mom murmured. And then: "Ptui!"

"What's the matter?" asked dad.

"It ain't no good," mom said sadly. "It's all gone to sugar." Groans were heard from the pickers, who had looked forward to a cool respite from sun and hard work.

Watermelon feasts, thank goodness, are still part of the vanishing rural scene, nor are cities far behind in their admiration for this fine fruit. But no one can convince me that what we buy in supermarkets, round as turtle eggs, picked green and trucked cross country, even come close to being as good as what we stole when we were kids.

DON'T ASK ME HOW, but I *know* my old man was taken on a snipe hunt when he was a kid. Otherwise, why did he chuckle and say, "Sure, go ahead," when I told him with great excitement that our nearest neighbors, George and James Harding, had invited me to hunt snipes with them?

It was 1945, near the end of our first year on the Pokero place, when those boys, both older than me (which impressed me even more) explained that snipe were delicious when baked in a pie but were elusive birds that could only be caught in bags at night. Immediately, I was abrim with interest, especially after James assured me they were worth all the hard work, and that even the crowned heads of Europe ate them.

"You mean kings and queens hunt snipes?"

"No, their servants get to have that fun," said George, a year older than fifteen-year-old James, who was three years older than me.

"Did you bring your tow sack?" asked George, and I held it up eagerly.

"How about your flashlight?" asked James. I held up a coal-oil lantern. "We ain't got a flashlight," I said. "Will a lantern do?"

"Ummmm," hesitated George. "What you think, James?" Such calculated discouragement only whetted my appetite. I'd heard about the mysteries and excitement of snipe hunting ever since our family reached the farm.

"Dang it!" I blurted. "I should've tried to borry a flashlight somewheres!"

James's smile wrapped me like a blanket. He was my favorite and enhanced his standing now by saying, "Oh, I reckon a lantern is all right. Like as not, if you tried to borry a flashlight from some farmer, he would want to go along, and we just got room for us—right, George?" With a warm smile, George nodded. Had I not been too old for such emotional displays, I would've hugged them both. Such friends don't grow on trees.

"Just be sure that lantern's full of oil," George cautioned. "Chances are, you'll be out late."

James said, "Right," in an odd voice, and then turned away and stared at the moon and breathed deeply for awhile. Then he turned back to George. "I just hope Billy can measure up. It ain't every city kid that can catch a snipe. You know how fast them birds fly."

Now it was George's turn to look away, but he ignored the moon and buried his face in a big red kerchief. His shoulders were shaking, normal enough considering the powerful nose-blowing that followed.

"Are they faster'n a quail?" I cried. "I've seen quail!"

"Are you kidding?" George said. "A quail is a snail compared to a snipe." He replaced his handkerchief. "Y'see, they're only out at night when other birds is roostin', so they ain't nothin' they can run into."

"Except the sack you'll be holdin'," James said. "But you got to hold the light proper, just over the sack, 'cause they move like bullets and only fly towards the light."

"Dang, dang, *dang!*" I cried in an ecstasy of profanity. "I sure hope I catch one!"

"Oh, you'll catch a bunch," George assured me.

James smiled warmly and added, "Ordinarily, we'd have a kid hold the light between his knees and use two sacks, but you're better'n that."

We got in their pickup and headed for the pond, about a mile across the pasture, as the moon shadows lengthened over the grassland. George and James positioned me near the pond and ran me through a lantern-and-sack drill and then drove away. I knew exactly where they were going, because they had told me.

"We're goin' out and beat the bushes," James had explained. "We'll wake the snipe up and get 'em headed your way. This could take quite a spell, so sit tight and be ready for them birds."

After about an hour, they still hadn't come back, and I wanted mightily to sit down. The lantern was as heavy as an anvil, and I hadn't seen foot nor feather of a snipe. But both brothers had warned me, "You got to stand here and keep your sack open and your lantern up. Those birds whiz past like arrows."

The sack, which was of burlap, weighed hardly anything at first, but half an hour later, it had grown to the weight of a full-sized car. I admit I cheated some, with both it and that infernal lantern. I had to, or else my arms would have dropped off.

"This snipe huntin' ain't all it's cracked up to be," I muttered, just as James, crashing through some far-away plum thickets with George, yelled, "Here comes six of 'em!" How he could count six birds in the dark mystified me, but I swept up my sack and lantern and stood like a miniature Colossus of Rhodes, while mosquitoes from the pond, out prospecting, found my richest vein and settled down to dine. Nary a snipe whizzed out of the dark, though.

Meanwhile, George and James started yelling again, but with a lot more energy and a few words mama didn't want me saying. I heard them floundering and crashing through the bushes, obviously in a hurry, plus some unidentifiable whoops. For sure, they had flushed a whole batch of snipes and were aiming them my way.

But again, no birds.

Not even after two hours. There was no more shouting or thrashing, either. But George and James were masters of concealment, and I was sure they were out there scaring up more birds. Fatigue and the warm summer night combined to make me sleepy, and at some point, I dozed off. The rest of the night millions of snipes bulleted past my open sack, always just out of reach, feathered dreams that would never come true.

I awoke cramped and cold, with a dead lantern. Well, it didn't matter. The moon was still high in the west and the pasture brighter than day. Trudging home, I told myself, "Okay, so you didn't get any snipes this time. There's always next time."

Next morning, I woke to hear Mrs. Harding talking to mom in the kitchen. She'd come for mom's poultice recipe. Seems that George and James had stumbled into a colony of yellow jackets in the plum thicket, and the critters hadn't taken kindly to the wake-up call. "Them boys is got more bumps than a prairie dog village," Mrs. Harding said.

Soon afterward, dad confided that I had now been initiated into the mysteries of country life, of which snipe hunts are one of the time-honored patriarchs.

THE POKERO PLACE, if memory serves, was a big rectangular one-story house built around the turn of the twentieth century and abused ever since. A porch with four stubby, square pillars faced the dirt road, and at the other end were chunky concrete steps with a galvanized-pipe handrail and two chinaberry trees.

We aren't talking the Ritz-Carlton here. It was a wood-frame house with a small opening in the south end, the end facing Big Beaver Creek, that allowed access to the underside. But because of black widow spiders and occasional marauding centipedes, we kids were told to stay out from under it. This was not the case with small animals, though, so dad tacked a piece of screen-door wire across the opening. Like I said somewhere, dad was no carpenter.

Sometimes I'd awaken at night on my pallet on the floor. Outside, the winds would be howling like all the fiends of hell, and raindrops the size of acorns would be pelting the leaky old structure. It occurred to me—often—that if a cyclone did hit us, we'd all be matchsticks. In the dimness, I always saw a motionless shadow at the window—my dad, awake and watching the blue norther that had roared up from nowhere, wondering if it would form a funnel cloud. Funny thing is, I can think back now over all those years and still feel the sense of security my old man evoked in me. My siblings slept the sleep of the innocent, but if dad awoke, I awoke, and he *always* awoke. He never made a sound, just stood there studying the sparkle of lightning that rolled huge billows of thunder after it.

At a certain point, if things got really bad, he would quietly awaken everybody, herd us together, and we'd march to the muddy old storm cellar out back. It was dug into the earth, with logs overhead that were covered by dirt, and inside it lived spiders and tiny frogs that liked moist places. There we huddled, the light from our red-painted lantern bouncing off jeweled jars of peaches and tomatoes. It may have seemed gravelike, but it protected us from one of the most powerful forces on earth.

How could anyone love such a crazy state? Yet my father did love it. My years in Oklahoma could be told in its storms, in the great winds that tore across the countryside cracking buildings and toppling trees. Such storms were frightening and magnificent, and many were deadly. When we lived near Bray, a small tornado devastated the fruit orchard a quarter mile from our aging shack of a house. Apples, plums, and pears littered the ground, and the trees looked like they'd been blasted by grenades. In one of them, a pear tree, was the strangest thing I ever saw: a yellow straw, no bigger than a wooden match, had been driven like a nail into the bark.

Stories abound of the might and strangeness of cyclones. Trains weighing hundreds of tons, for instance, have been lifted like paper chains. I didn't believe such stories until years later, when I went to Wichita Falls, Texas, to do a rodeo story soon after the devastating tornado of 1979. Boxcars littered the plains like children's blocks in an eerie tableau of the twister's power.

Two years later, in Bartlesville, Oklahoma, I saw what a twister could do to concrete, steel, and brick. A dozen brick and concrete buildings were reduced to rubble that night, and scores of cars and trucks were crumpled or sent tumbling along the pavement when the twister struck them. My oldest son Chris, then fourteen, was living with me at the time. From the basement where we huddled, we heard the rushing *whoo-o-o-om* of the tornado. Suddenly, to my surprise and terror, my son bolted up the stairs. I could feel my hair turning gray, or could have, if I'd had enough.

"Chris!" I screamed. "What the hell are you doing? Get back here!"

Glumly, he returned, telling me that he "just wanted to see a tornado because in California we don't have any." But Chris was mistaken—California (and every other state) does have tornadoes. Somebody once figured out it has an average of 5 per year. The champ is Texas, with a whopping 131 in an average year; surprisingly, Florida has 48—just 5 less than overblown Oklahoma.

LIFE ON THE POKERO FARM—that time at least—went reasonably well. We weathered a hard winter, dad's winter wheat survived, and we had a good stand of cotton by late May. I was in school and had made a few rural acquaintances—including a self-important little jackass named Bobby Fisher, the son of the only rich farmer in those parts. Their farm was two miles up the road, and they had something nobody else did—a telephone. Bobby and I hated each other but pretended we didn't.

One spring day in May 1945, dad came home from the stock sale and said, "I run into old man Dootzman at the sale barn, and he's got fifty acres he wants turned. I said okay, you'd do it."

Henry Dootzman was a German who had a pig farm half a mile down the road. Calling it a farm was being charitable—it was more like a charnel yard. On summer days, or any days, the smell of rotting flesh hit your nose like a hammer. Kids riding the wood-sided yellow school bus that had to pass Dootzman's place called it the "Boneyard," as indeed it was. When the wind was just right, there was a mighty rush to close the windows—not that it did any good.

"Agghhh!" gagged boys all over the bus.

"Ee-yewww!" gasped the girls.

"Mother of Jesus!" groaned the bus driver, pinching his nose.

The Boneyard existed because Dootzman raised hogs and cows, and when a cow, hog, or horse died, he simply tied it to a tractor and dragged it into the pigpen for the pigs to eat. There, to the delight of the pigs, it rotted for a very long time—fine for them, but not for anyone passing by. Palisades of thigh bones and forests of ribs littered the corral, white or gray depending on how much they had rotted. The pigpen covered three acres and held about one hundred black and white Hampshire hogs at any given time, because Dootzman's sows were always farrowing, and no sooner would he take a load to the auction barn than more would be born. Those pigs required lots of protein, which meant the Dootzmans also shopped around for dead animals—any large kind they could get for free and haul home. Stinking carcasses were therefore always in the pen, with their bones scattered around, much like kindling. Dootzman walked unconcernedly through this open-air cemetery, carrying buckets of corn for the hogs.

If a cow had a good hide, Henry and his boys skinned her out. There was always a need for strips of leather on the farm, so the inside of the barn had any number of cured hides hanging on the wall. I'd seen Dootzman do amazing things, like using leather strips wound around an axle as bearings on a wagon that should have been junked years earlier.

All those bones lying around wasn't the worst of things. When the hog pen was upwind of the kitchen, the breezes blew the smell right into it—an event I was soon to have firsthand knowledge of.

"Am I getting paid?" I asked dad.

"Paid?" he snorted. "'Course you're gettin' paid! You'll eat your share of half a beef he's givin' me for plowin' his field."

"Mules or tractor?"

"Henry said you could drive his new Ford-Ferguson if you promise not to break it."

Now, this was more like it. The war was only waiting on the Japanese to be over, and old man Dootzman was one of the very first to have a newly manufactured tractor. "How many days you think it'll take?"

"Days? I'm talkin' about night plowin'."

Night plowing? Yikes, I'd never plowed at night, and in 1945, it was a whole lot harder than it is now. The tractor lights were better than moonlight, but there the convenience ended. Still, it would be an adventure. I would start each evening after supper and plow till midnight and probably finish in two days, or three at the most.

It was nearly suppertime when Dootzman clattered into the yard in his old pickup. "The boy can eat with us, J. W.," he said. "Get an early start that way." And away we chugged.

Now, the Dootzmans were Catholics and had so many kids (thirteen) that the old lady spent most of her time in the kitchen—that is, when she wasn't in the hospital giving birth. She was as short and wide as Mr. Dootzman was lean and wiry. I knew I'd made a mistake the minute I sat down. Mrs. Dootzman brought big flat pans of cornbread, and twenty-eight pieces went to plates filled with twenty-eight ladlefuls of pinto beans. I saw immediately that these were serious eaters, solemnly addressing the victuals, no conversation or laughter.

A huge platter of fried beef appeared and just as quickly disappeared. The only sound was the noise of four hundred forty-eight teeth chewing. My thirty-two weren't included because I was feeling sick to my stomach. Mrs. Dootzman had opened the right half of the kitchen window for air, and an odor blew in from the hog pens that would gag a maggot. My stomach rolled like overalls in a washer, my bile tried to climb up my throat, and my gag reflex kicked in with such a vengeance it took all my willpower to halt it.

The incredibly foul smell enveloped everybody at the table in a green mist, or so I imagined, and it got stronger by the second. I glanced into the kitchen and saw Mrs. Dootzman calmly ladling up gravy to bring to the table. I looked at the other Dootzmans. Their heads were bent, and they were shoveling in victuals at a great rate. Not one appeared to notice the horrible stench pouring into the house (which itself smelled like a tomb). My mouth suddenly filled with hot saliva, a sure sign that I was about to be sick. I had to get out of there before I added something to the banquet that no one expected.

"Excuse me," I mumbled. "I think I'll go check the tractor and plow. Make sure everything's okay." And I skidded my chair back and exited as fast as I could without seeming frantic. The Dootzmans paid no attention. They ate on, only now Mrs. Dootzman had joined them—but not before opening the other half of the window. I ran out behind the barn and heaved until my innards hurt.

THE FORD-FERGUSON was a small, gray tractor with "Finger Touch" hydraulic lifters on its two plowshares—the high-tech wonder of postwar America, but nothing like the banks of plows on today's monster tractors. It wasn't comfortable, either, being too light and too bouncy. In fact, unless farmers made and used cement weights, the whole front end could rear up if a plow sank too deep. But I stayed on that riddled steel seat and did my job.

Night plowing is windy and lonely, and the danger of falling asleep and dropping under the tractor wheels is real. But kids did what they were told in those days and in fact were proud of being given a chance to act like grown-ups.

A full moon rode overhead, surrounded by a gravel of stars spattering the sky. Henry's two older sons—both humorless men, or so I thought—were on tractors elsewhere, so I wouldn't be seeing anybody on my lonely journey round and round the fifty-acre field. The oldest Dootzman boy, Thomas, was serving in Europe with the army.

On top of that (as you may have guessed), the hired boy got the field that skirted the Boneyard, with all its reeking carcasses. Round and round, I plowed in my unending circle of stink, and even with a cold wind, I was practically choking. At last there came a moment when my nose, outraged by such treatment, turned off and refused to smell anymore, which brought some relief. But I could still see, and each time I passed that ghostly graveyard and the bleak old barn, the scraggly trees seemed to claw at me, and their leaves rubbed like nesting snakes. What with the full moon making all sorts of patterns as it moved across the sky, I was able to work up a healthy feeling of spookiness. The little tractor droned on, the plow whispered through the earth, the wind moaned, and I was one lonely boy.

Even the pigs had gone to bed, though how they could stand each other's breath, I couldn't imagine. I wondered if the Dootzman boys were feeling the presence of ghosts—the spirits of the bovine, equine, and porcine dead whose bones now decorated the pens. I doubted it. Fear and laughter are cousins, and I'd never seen them so much as crack a smile about anything.

The moon was slowly crumpling towards the west as midnight came and went. Soon there would be only starlight, and starlight can make the simplest objects change shape or seem to move. The tractor lights, canted down towards the furrows, didn't help much since they made the front wheels seem to lunge forward like shadowy hands. No doubt about it, I was in the realm of the dead, and just because it was an animal graveyard didn't ease my mind any. I hoped my old man, warm in his bed, was at least having nightmares because I sure was. As the Ford-Ferguson moaned along, I wished I was anywhere but here, doing anything but this.

Alone in the dark, I became a great surgeon, operating on the field's flesh, noticing the dark hulk of the barn, watching fence posts catch my headlights by the Boneyard, seeing the shadowy form of a dead cow rise up and start trotting towards me . . .

"Wa-a-a-u-g-h!"

I don't remember the exact sound I made as I bailed off that tractor, but that's close enough. Hell was on my heels, my heart was in my throat, and I wished my ass was in West Texas. I hit the furrows like a sack of grain, desperate to escape the terrifying apparition. *But my legs wouldn't move!* Like someone in a nightmare, my limbs had turned to water. With another screech, I turned my head to see how close the corpse was and whether it was gaining.

That's when I saw the two older Dootzman boys wrapped around a fence post in helpless laughter. The tractor lights caught the crumpled cowhide at their feet. They had taken it from the barn for their lousy joke. I was done for, and I knew it. Soon the story would be everywhere. I would be the butt of jokes all over Oklahoma.

But before that could occur, something wonderful came down the pike that drove all thought of their joke from the Dootzmans' minds. The war in Europe ended on May 8—and they got word that their son Thomas was safe. He would finish his remaining time in the army and be discharged in California in a few weeks.

Dad got his beef. But I never ate a bite of it. The memory of dinner at the Dootzmans' was too strong.

LATE MAY and early June did for Oklahoma what my imagination could not, and our homely old lease was suddenly as pretty as a painting. Winter's rains and snows always funneled water from the clay road into our "yard"—actually a half acre of space between the house and the barn—so that in February, a real loblolly was in place, churned up by tractor wheels and the hooves of horses and mules. But there was little rain through June, July, and August, so that area was soon as hard as a highway.

But for 320 acres around this red pancake, every kind of flower bloomed, and every kind of weed, too. The roadside ditches were dazzled by the amethyst blossoms of chicory. Wild sunflowers grew so tall they made a jungle for pigs to tunnel through, and we kids dried their long straight stalks to hurl at each other as spears. Daisies coated the pastures like curds of cottage cheese, green chinaberries (waxy yellow in the fall) grew on our twin trees, and along Big Beaver Creek, half a mile away, possum grape vines were putting out tiny green BBs that made tasty jams and jellies when they turned purple in the fall. Dandelion puffs pirouetted on the summer breeze like tiny ballerinas.

It was the perfect time to catch June bugs, tie a thread to one of their legs, and let them buzz around and around like almond-sized ornithopters. Many years later, I would teach that same trick to my citified kids, and they loved it. It doesn't hurt the bugs, which are eventually freed, and the boys thought it was a capital idea. One summer when they couldn't come for a visit, I captured several June bugs and mailed them in a box to my young sons in California. From what I was told, there was great excitement when they opened it, for the bugs escaped and began whizzing around the house. The boys were delighted with their miniature air force, but Rosie, their mother—terrified of flying things ever since a bat once tangled in her hair—required a sedative.

AT TWELVE, being the only kid old enough to work (Glenda was six and just learning to help mom, David was five, and Helen was barely four), one of my jobs was to go to the creek each evening and round up the milk cows. I did this on foot because I didn't yet have a horse I could ride. Big Beaver Creek was a typical Oklahoma creek, regularly flooded, choked with briars and vines, and with good bottomland overwhelmed by a vicious plant called johnsongrass. Farmers hated this weed, which was practically impossible to hoe out when its bamboolike tentacles started strangling corn, maize, or cotton. It took a special tool, a heavy triangular grubbing hoe, to even cut its tangled roots, and swinging this brute all day made your shoulders want to resign from your body.

Related to sorghum, johnsongrass was named after William Johnston, the idiot who imported it for cattle graze from the Mediterranean in the 1880s. Today, there's a herbicide that kills it, but in 1945 we used plows, cultivators, grubbing hoes, and an endless supply of elbow grease. The grass, whose bamboo-tough pencil-sized stalks can grow eight feet high, was rarely defeated—its knotted roots spread like tentacles below the surface. Some farmers, finding an arable field infested, simply gave up and let it go to pasture. The grass was only moderately useful for hay and no favorite of grazing cattle except when young and green.

I'm telling you all this because I want you to be able to see the field of battle that's shaping up. To my right was tree-shadowed Beaver Creek with its pools, thorns, and poison ivy. Ahead grew a jungle of johnsongrass. Laced by animal trails and flanked by yellow-green walls, it easily hid the bovines. The milk cows were always led by an old pied cow, and predictably, dad called her "Old Pied." She later fell victim to wolves. Now, camouflaged by the tall grass, I could hear them moving and chewing but couldn't pinpoint their location.

"Hooo-eeee, Pied!" I called. "Come on, girl!"

Nothing.

"Hooo-eeeeeee, Pied!"

Still nothing. Suddenly I heard a rustling coming from behind me and jumped aside, half burying myself in the grass (which was festive with ticks and chiggers)—just as a roly-poly, black-and-white shape came trundling along the trail. My heart did a flip-flop. *A polecat!* I had never seen a skunk up close before, but some of my new school chums informed me that skunk pelts were in demand by the military, which paid fifty cents apiece—a king's ransom in those days. They used the fur in arctic regions because it wouldn't frost over. True or not, greed made me believe the story, and when I saw the skunk, I went immediately into a chase-and-capture mode.

"Zowie!" I shouted, and the chase was on—but not before I grabbed a handy limb lying in the trail. Away sped the skunk, and away sped me, down one grass-walled trail and up another. *Fifty cents!* I hadn't held that much money in my life! Finally, I got close enough to swing my stick. The blow landed, the skunk curled up, and I reached down and retrieved my little cash cow by its tail.

I would not have been dumb enough, even as a city kid, to do that if a school chum hadn't promised me that no skunk can spray if you hold it up by its tail. This bit of wisdom was right in there with the formula that promised a bird couldn't fly if you sprinkled salt on its tail. But I went for it.

I was congratulating myself on being rich when the skunk shuddered, and my head took off for parts unknown. Not only did I drop the skunk, which left the premises, but I staggered around retching and coughing, my eyes streaming tears and my nose filled with battery acid. I couldn't breathe, I couldn't sneeze, I could only flop around in the grass and wonder how soon I could die, and why didn't it hurry and happen, because, oh, how I wanted to. I even got religion for a moment, groaning "Oh, God, let me die!" before stumbling to my feet and reeling toward the creek.

I cannonballed into the muddy stream, clothes, shoes, and all and started going down, down, down. Instantly, I realized that the awful fumes were not so easily unseated. I blew back to the surface like a small whale, rolled around, and scrubbed my face and body with mud—nothing helped! My torment went on and on. I vomited, washed it off, and crawled weakly back to the bank.

At last, when I was sure my heart could not last another second, my tortured nose went into paralysis, or a death lock, or maybe even kidney trouble. All I know is that it finally stopped sizzling and shut down completely. Not knowing when the assault might start again, I got to my feet and began looking for the cows—not easy, because my eyes were swollen to narrow slits. I was sicker than a calf with scours, so it was a wonderful sight to suddenly run into the herd, led by Old Pie, heading sedately homeward. I grabbed the tail of the last cow so I wouldn't get lost and stumbled after them with my swollen eyes streaming tears.

I hoped that the awful odor would dissipate on the way home, but forget that. Even though I couldn't smell myself, I knew others could, and as I stumbled toward the house (the cows having opted for hay in the milk barn), I spied my family leaving the other side, thinking an invasion of skunks was coming.

"Great God almighty!" my dad shouted. "What the hell have you been up to now?" He sure could ask penetrating questions. Had he lost his sense of smell? But at least there was comfort in the fact that he wasn't about to establish the closeness necessary for corporal punishment.

"I ran into a skunk," I wailed. "It wasn't my fault!"

One thing kids learn early is the difference between a real lie and a white lie. A white lie has value, because it can keep you out of the woodshed, whereas a real lie—if detected—can get you into it.

"Of all the *ignorant* things I ever saw!" dad fumed. Behind him, mom nodded her head grimly while Glenda, David, and Helen simply looked on, owl-eyed and holding their noses. My almost-new overalls were ruined, and I was dumped unceremoniously in the stock tank, which was colder than a polar bear's nose. Mom made alternate advances and retreats, holding her own nose and a washcloth saturated with lye soap. Not that it did any good. Nothing did. For the entire week following the encounter, I had to sit in the back of the school bus with all the windows down, as well as in the back of the classroom, while the other kids clustered up front. It's a wonder I didn't catch pneumonia, which I believe my schoolmates would have approved of.

But on the horizon, unknown to me, lurked a kind of vindication. Not too far down the road, dad would have his own adventure with a skunk. One day, I was tossing bales of hay off a wagon and stacking them in the barn when I heard shouting. The hay bales and barn walls muffled the sounds, so I paid little mind at first, figuring my siblings were playing a game.

Then I heard it more clearly. It was my old man, yelling, "Lorraine! *Lorraine!*" There was fright in every syllable. Now, I've said my dad was the strong, silent type, who made very little noise, but I didn't mean to imply that he didn't know how. Obviously, he was in some kind of peril, so I bailed out of the loft and ran to the front of the barn where I could see the house fifty yards away. I quickly realized there wasn't a thing I could do—or actually wanted to.

Mom stood on the big concrete steps, and dad, his skinny legs pumping, was nearing the corner of the house. He sounded like he was trying to wheeze every cigarette he'd ever smoked out of his lungs. "Lorraine, get the shotgun!" he yelled. "Hurry, I'm runnin' outta breath!"

Now, this was interesting. Even the chickens and the big old rooster that ruled them had stopped clucking and were looking and listening. Then I saw the mother skunk, her roly-poly shape racing along behind my old man—and gaining. You'd be surprised how fast a mama skunk can run when she's motivated.

I knew what had happened. The flimsy piece of screen dad had tacked over the house's end vent was loose, and the skunk, probably with small kits, had made herself and them at home. When dad hunkered down to tack the screen back, she objected. The results were being played out before every creature in the farmyard.

How long dad had been picking them up and putting them down I didn't know. He was huffing and puffing like a switch engine, had lost his straw hat, and now shouted again for mom to throw him the .20-gauge. "She's a *hydrophobia* skunk!" he hollered, although there was no way he could know that. I figured the skunk was just mad and protecting her babies, like all animal mothers did. Dad was lucky she wasn't a grizzly.

On his next revolution, mom gripped the galvanized-pipe banister with one hand and leaned out with the shotgun in the other, held by its stock. Dad grabbed and missed.

"God*damn* it!" he roared, galloping off again with the snarling, spitting skunk right on his heels. Then something else occurred to him. "Make sure it's loaded!" came his voice from around the house's far corner. Well, it wasn't, so mom had to run inside, find a shell, and load one into the 1890 Remington single-shot. Out she came again—and this time dad grabbed the gun by the barrel. Now, though, he was in imminent peril of being bitten. The skunk didn't smoke, was nowhere near as tired as dad, and was gaining with every hop. From the barn door, I watched as dad cocked the hammer, turned, aimed, and pulled the trigger.

Click! A misfire.

"*Lorraine,* gimme another shell!" he screamed. Away he went again, but now the mama skunk was literally snapping at his brogans. One way or another, this was the last spiral. The *tableau vivant* had to end, because dad was so winded his wheezing could be heard in Tulsa. Mom reached out the shell to dad, who loaded it on the run, turned—and blew the skunk away with a charge of number 4 shot. For some reason, she didn't fire her own weapon, which was a blessing. Dad stumbled to the steps and sat down, wheezing like a broken bellows. He hadn't run that hard or that far in years.

Mom's twitching lips told me that she was fighting not to laugh. Dad ejected the spent shell, then looked curiously at the one that hadn't fired. He slid it into the shotgun, set the butt on the steps, and for some reason pulled the trigger. The .20-gauge roared, kicked out of his hands, and bounced down the steps. Dad let out an enraged bellow. "Goddamn it to hell! What *else* can happen?" The shotgun's ancient firing pin hadn't hit the first shell hard enough.

Standing in the barn door, I wanted to yell, "Hey, dad! Remember the time that polecat sprayed me down by Big Beaver Creek?" Of course, I didn't say it, because he was fatigued from running and just getting over a scare, and he might be a little lacking in the humor department right then.

ONE MORNING in June 1945, a new pickup rolled into the yard. At the wheel was Bobby Fisher's father, Hoke, looking solemn, and beside him, Bobby, looking self-important. He was the most obnoxious twelve-year-old I ever knew.

As Mr. Fisher went inside to talk to mom and dad, Bobby sidled up to me and said, "Betcha don't know why we're here."

"Betcha I don't care, either."

Bobby was undeterred. "We're delivering a death message," he said importantly, sliding his hands into his pockets. "We got the call on our telephone this morning."

Our telephone. The little rat. I'd caught his sneering inflection, but I was curious.

"Who is it that died?"

"Henry and Wanda Dootzman's son. The one that was in the war."

And so he had. The news hit me like a blow, because I liked Thomas even though I'd only met him a few times. While waiting for shipment home from Northern California, the Dootzmans' eldest, a decorated soldier who had fought all over Europe and survived, went fishing on a high Sierra lake with a buddy. Somehow their boat capsized, and both of them drowned in the paralyzingly cold water.

I left Bobby Fisher standing with his self-important hands in his self-important pockets and went out to the barn. There, I sat on a hay bale and stared at the stanchions without seeing them for a long time. Finally, I heard vehicles starting and knew that mom, dad, Bobby, and Mr. Fisher were en route to tell the Dootzmans the bad news and try to comfort them. I walked outside. It was summer, but the world seemed gray. I stared across the fields toward Big

Beaver Creek. It was still the same world, but nothing made any sense. It would not be the last time in my life that I would reach that conclusion, and usually it was a death that prompted it. What good was a God that couldn't even save one drowning hero?

SUMMER HAD MADE a difference in the ugliness of southwest Oklahoma. The pastures were green and high with grass, through which the cows made their irregular trails, and the farm pond teemed with bullfrogs the size of guinea hens. Big Beaver Creek, only half a mile away, featured fish and turtles, and there were plenty of squirrels, for anyone wanting them.

The creek washed out new pools during spring floods, and this time it had left a fine swimming hole. Being busy in the fields, I only got to try it on Sunday. Uncle Tom (whose full name was Thomas Pleasant Childress) occasionally brought his wife Thelma and some of their brood for a visit. That meant my cousins Jimmy and Johnny, who were near my age, would be available for mischief.

On one visit, they taught me how to "smoke" grapevine. Later, they stole some of their dad's Prince Albert and rolled it into corn shuck cigarettes—anything to be "grown-up." Those kids could inhale from the age of ten, but the last I heard, the only inhaling they did was from oxygen bottles. They had to lug them around because they had emphysema.

But that long-ago day, at their urging, I sucked in a big lungful of corn shuck/tobacco smoke and fell into such an agonized fit of coughing I almost died.

"Dang you guys!" I yelled, when I finally could. "You nearly killed me!" They just smirked, and to demonstrate how you can get used to frying your windpipe, they sucked in big lungfuls of smoke and didn't cough a lick. In time, associating with Jimmy and Johnny led me to an eighteen-year tobacco addiction, the worst mistake of my life. It took me three attempts before I finally rid myself of that stupid habit forever. Today, if I even smell someone smoking, it turns my stomach.

WHEN I WASN'T being dad's auxiliary mule, I briefly attended classes at a crappy school in Bray, Oklahoma, where the emphasis, as always, was on sports. And that's enough about Bray.

I also went to school for awhile in Cement, Oklahoma. I have a great memory of that place. One night in front of the soda fountain, a school bully thought he'd aggravate a local boy who, in the parlance of the day, was "addled." The kid was probably just severely tongue-tied, but in any case, he had a tough time making understandable sounds. He was a husky fellow, but not as big as the jock.

"What a bozo!" laughed the athlete, making faces at the boy and mocking him. His toadies laughed dutifully. This went on for some minutes, while the boy's attempts at speech became ever more agitated. Then with lightning speed, the kid leaped in and landed a punch to the jock's face that knocked him down. With his nose bleeding, he looked dazedly at the boy. Obviously, the kid knew something about boxing, probably taught to him because his parents knew he'd be teased.

The kid danced around the fallen bully, his fists raised. But the guy didn't want any more to do with him, and he quickly left. I'd had my own encounters with jocks and bullies, often one and the same, and I went home happy as a lark. Poetic justice rarely happens, but that just makes it more delicious when it does.

INVARIABLY, WE sharecropped a red-dirt farm so infertile nobody else would take it, and this was partly true of the Pokero place. But where most farmers saw red dirt, my father saw rainbows, and he couldn't wait to plow the first field—with me, of course, plowing the second, third, fourth, and so on. Row cropping, in those days, was still primitive, with real manure instead of manufactured chemicals, and with tractors sharing field chores with horses and mules. On the days I was in school, I'd get home to hear dad hollering, "Get out of yer school clothes and into some work clothes and hitch up them mules!" Soon, I'd be stumbling down furrows behind a harrow. Sometimes, though, I got to ride the old John Deere dad bought at a farm sale, which was more to my liking.

In late summer, dad's fifty-acre field was heavy with grain, so he contacted a neighbor who agreed to bring his thresher and "thrash" the oats for a share—standard practice at the time. The day they harvested dad's oats, I was full of excitement, because this was something new. So were Helen, David, and Glenda—although they were still too small to be allowed around large equipment. Labor swapping was common among small, farmers, and the crew had come the day before to cut, tie, and stack dad's oats in shocks. By day's end, the field looked like it was full of little golden tepees. These would be wagoned to the thresher where the grain would be separated and loaded into trucks. The chaff would be blown into a thirty-foot mountain of yellow straw.

I could hear the thresher coming from a long way off, a huge machine made of galvanized metal with four iron wheels, built in the 1920s. Such machines are mostly in agricultural museums today. The thresher rumbled down the clay road, pulled by a Minneapolis-Moline tractor. Squeaking and swaying, it entered the gate to a field of oats that rippled in the wind like golden foil. There, its owner carefully positioned it so wagons could bring the sheaves alongside and throw them into the metal maw. Then huge flails turned with a *whoo-o-o-mm* like an approaching tornado. Of course, none of this could happen until the owner unrolled a huge, flat belt on the ground between the thresher's grinding wheel and the tractor's power-takeoff pulley. He then lifted the cumbersome belt onto both pulleys and inched the tractor backwards to tighten it. At the proper moment, he engaged the clutch, and the long belt began moving, slapping as it picked up speed, and finally settled into a slithering snake that could eat a hand if you weren't cautious. The owner held a stick of belt dressing against it, and soon the sound of a giant vacuum cleaner filled the air.

Inching closer to where two men were making adjustments, I tried to see the howling machinery inside. Suddenly, one of the men shouted over the din of spinning gears, "Did you hear 'bout that kid over in Chickasha who fell into one of these things?" I never saw him wink at his companion.

"Sure did," the other man said. "They wasn't enough left of that boy to fill a coffee can with."

"They was so much blood, the newspaper said, that it just soaked the grain," the first one continued. "It was all over the thrasher and the ground and in the gears. Completely ruined the wheat. Couldn't even use it for hog feed."

"Blood, you say? That ain't nothin' to the guts—small intestines I think they were—that got all tangled inside the thrasher. I don't think they'll ever be able to thrash grain with that machine again."

One of them must've seen my green face and horrified expression, because they busted out laughing, which was heard by the others even over the roar of the machine's innards. I felt like a complete fool.

Just then, dad hollered, "Bill! Get that bucket full o' water from the well, and keep us watered, y'hear?" As I picked up the galvanized pail with its enameled dipper and headed for the well, I heard the first sawmill sound as the machine, whirling at top speed, bit into the sheaves of grain being thrown into it. A golden stream shot forty feet from a metal spout to begin a chaff pile that would eventually be as big as a house. That meant feed for the cows, who ate around the bottom and left a mushroom shape, and fun for us kids, who would slide down it.

Meanwhile, as the threshing got underway, the farm wives were cooking up a big harvest dinner, which would be ready to serve at the crack of noon. The women would bring pots of pinto beans, bowls of mashed potatoes, a cauldron of cream gravy, mounds of biscuits, and platter after platter of steaks, chicken, and pork chops. There were twenty or thirty men to feed, and it took plenty of food. The dishes and pans were set on long planks with sawhorses for legs and bed sheets for tablecloths.

Two chinaberry trees, common in Oklahoma, grew a few yards from the concrete steps leading into the house, and the tables reposed in their shade. The women would bring the food down the stairs to the table, and the men would eat, rest awhile, and then go back to work. The kids and womenfolk waited until they were gone—and to a hungry kid, that seemed like eternity.

About an hour before noon, mom told me to tell dad I was lugging my last water bucket until after dinner. "She needs me to crank the ice cream freezer," I told my sweating father, and he said, "Okay, go on then, but get back on this bucket after we eat. These men need water."

I went back and watched mom put cream, sugar, egg yolks, crushed pecans, and vanilla in two big hand-operated freezers. It would make about four gallons of ice cream, and if we kids were lucky, there'd be some left for us. But it would have to be luck. I've lived a lifetime since, but I've never seen any group that could eat like those harvest crews. Some of them didn't stop with seconds— they went on to thirds and fourths.

"Don't put no ice in them freezers till they're already eatin'," mom cautioned. "It'll freeze up fast when I add the salt to the ice, and you want it cold and thick for the men."

The kitchen was a circus of bustling women and wonderful smells—although how they could work in such a small space with only one wood range, I never figured out. There were pies cooling, two-layer cakes, fried chicken, pitchers of iced tea, pork chops, steaks, potatoes, gravy, turnip greens, corn, and green beans. Hot biscuits and cornbread crossed vapor trails and made me so hungry I almost fainted. There were a lot more viands, but that will give you an idea.

"Here they come!" a woman whooped, and soon a dozen grimy men were turning the outdoor wash pan's water black, tossing and refilling it, and attacking the dirt on their faces and necks with Lava soap and wash rags. Overhead, the sun gleamed like a white-hot coal. Threshing was hot work.

The food was on the table, and I was hunkered at one corner of the big concrete steps cranking the freezer. Those steps always made me think that they had too much concrete left from making the foundation, so they tried to stretch it and make a porch. Anyway, they were big steps for a bungalow.

My brother and sisters looked out at the scene from behind the window screens, more hungry than curious. What a feast! I've never eaten better than at a threshing-day dinner. The men went through those victuals like geese through a gate, devoured their ice cream, and went back to work. The water-toter would join them as soon as he'd eaten, which I proceeded to do with my brother and sisters while the women talked and filled their own plates.

At day's end, with the work done, accounts were settled and the men went wearily homeward. My siblings and I could look out on a field of golden stubble and a chaff pile that resembled a custard mountain. I swear, if I ever see a chaff pile again, I'll ask the owners to let me slide down it.

HOW A PERFECT KID like me could ever hook up with a pair like Jimmy and Johnny Childress, I never figured out. Looking back, I tell myself that surely I didn't suffer every time I was with them; that we must have had harmless fun at least once. But the more I ponder, the more I doubt it. Those two simply thrived on mischief.

One weekend Uncle Tom and Aunt Thelma had trusted their old Model A, with its baling-wire spark plug wires, to make the thirty-five mile trip from their sharecrop farm in Cache, Oklahoma, to dad's. I'd ridden in that relic. It steamed like a switch engine in a rail yard. If it stopped steaming, Uncle Tom looked for any handy ditch or stock pond and filled the radiator, no matter how muddy the water was. I wondered how much Oklahoma red clay was fused to the inside of the engine block.

Anyway, Jimmy, Johnny, and I were messing around inside the barn, and I could see my cousins getting bored. "Ain't there *nothin'* to do around here?" grumbled Jimmy.

"Well, you been here enough you ought to know," I said. "How about Big Beaver Creek?"

"Nah, it's still too cold," Johnny said. He had been poking around an old door, trying to pull it open. "What's in here?"

"That's an old grain bin," I said. "We don't use it. The oats in it is moldy and rotten and packed down solid."

Johnny and Jimmy looked at each other.

"Bumblebees!" they yelled in unison, with devilish grins. "I'll bet that ol' grain pile is full o' hives! And they ain't nothin' better than bumblebee honey."

All I knew about bumblebees was that they were slow, built nests underground, made extra-sweet honey, and could sting in a highly professional manner. Big, fuzzy black bees with yellow stripes, their heavy buzzing gives them their name.

"C'mon!" said Johnny, heading for our trash pile. There, he dug up and flattened three Valvoline motor oil cans, punctured them with nail holes, and nailed them to wooden laths. The result was a large metal swatter.

"What's that for?" I asked.

"You'll see," said Jimmy, as we walked back to the granary. There, he and Johnny pried the door off, and we stepped inside the musty room. It was lit by bars of light streaming in through holes in the roof. Johnny grinned at me.

"You're in for the best time you ever had!" he said. "We're gonna stir up the bees, and when they come out, we swat 'em! It's like they're bombers, and we're the gun crews!"

I showed my enthusiasm for the idea right off.

"Listen," I said. "I ain't never done this before. I need to learn how to do it right, so I'll just stand outside and watch through the cracks."

"Chicken!"

Grudgingly, I took a post inside the granary door, figuring that if worst came to worst, I could at least escape ahead of my cousins. Johnny edged toward the smelly mound of darkened oats, holding a piece of plank. "Get ready!" he said. "I'm gonna dig 'em out!"

"Maybe there won't be any in there," I said nervously.

"They'll be plenty," Jimmy said. "Hell's bells, they're so slow you can dodge 'em and still knock 'em dead!"

"Here goes!" yelled Johnny. He plunged the plank into the eight-foot mound and reamed it around. For a moment, nothing happened. Then a dark cloud swarmed out of the grain, more bumblebees than any of us had ever seen. Hundreds, maybe millions, each one eager to rebuke us for our bad manners. Even as he readied his tin swatter, Johnny was hit—and hit again.

"Yow!" he yelled, "Ow!"

He was swatting madly, knee-deep in moldy grain, but had barely touched the tip of the bee-berg. Soon the granary was wall-to-wall humming as the yellow-banded bugs defended their turf. Robbing a bee tree had never been like this. Smoked bees mostly just dozed. Bumblebees mostly just stung.

"Ow! Ow! Ow!" Jimmy yelped, flailing at—and missing—angry, incoming bees. I stood frozen by the door, trying to see anything coming at me through the sun-slatted shadows. The fact that I didn't move probably saved me.

"They's too many!" Johnny hollered, even though he'd started connecting and several bees had thunked against his swatter. "We ain't got a chance!"

"Let's get outta here!" yelled Jimmy, as more bumblebees breached his defenses. That was all I needed, and I was out of the granary and running hard, hoping the bees would stay put. My cousins threw down their Valvoline oil-can swatters and came galloping after. Happily, the bees didn't follow.

Outside, Johnny looked at his brother and said angrily, "You and your smart-aleck ideas!"

"*Me?* You're the one that said how easy it'd be! Shore as hell wasn't nothin' easy on my end!"

Johnny had a quarter-sized red circle with a white center on his neck and four more like it on his face. They looked like boils ready to pop. Poor Jimmy was even worse off. He was in real pain but too stubborn to cry. Biting off a chunk of Brown's Mule, Jimmy chewed it into a poultice and daubed it on their stings. Tobacco was supposed to be good for bee stings—another folk medicine myth, though maybe it had a placebo effect.

I've never fought bumblebees again, and that's been over half a century. Years later, when I came home on furlough, mom told me that dad had recently plowed through an underground hive. She still couldn't talk about it without laughing.

"He was plowin' a new garden plot with the tractor," she said. "I was takin' him some ice tea when all of a sudden he stood up on the tractor and started wavin' his arms like they had motors on 'em. I thought he was tellin' me to hurry up, but then he jumped down and started runnin' towards me, still wavin' his arms around! They was a cloud of somethin' around him, and he was slappin' hisself pretty good. That's when I knew he'd plowed into a bumblebee nest in the chaff from last year."

Mom said dad whizzed past her like she was a tree in a meadow. She heard a *pop!*—and his feet flew up like he'd hit an invisible limb. He landed, in mom's words, "right on his skinny butt!" A bumblebee in a kamikaze attack dove into dad's forehead with enough force to drive its stinger into the next county.

"He wasn't in no hurry to get up, neither," mom chortled. "I ain't never laughed so hard in my life. He had a knot on his forehead as big as a duck egg!"

I WOULDN'T HAVE SAID so as a kid, but my parents, for all their mental quirks and emotional knots, were perfect for a son determined to be a writer. Not because they encouraged it (dad urged me to be a barber, and mom wanted me to be a country entertainer) but because they and the life we led made such darn good copy.

I'd better explain, or defend, that "country entertainer" remark. Dad actually made a good living for awhile during the war as a copper miner, and one day he gave in to mom's insistence and bought me a Gene Autry guitar, complete with a painted Gene in the saddle of a rearing Champion. It was the most impressive $10 guitar I'd ever seen, and I wish I had it now. It would be worth some money on the *Antiques Road Show*.

I was twelve at the time, and by the time I was sixteen, I could play three chords with energy, but I was wondering why I didn't sound like a country entertainer. It mystified me, because I had grown up on country music and always tried to sing like the country singers. But if practice made perfect, why wasn't I a star? I spent a lot of time chording while admiring the likes of Tex Ritter, T. Texas Tyler, and maybe even Texarkana, Texas. All I knew was that there were a lot of Tex's in the field.

That was a drawback for a kid born in the Oklahoma Ozarks. Who ever heard of a singer called T. Oklahoma Tyler or Oklahoma Ritter? I couldn't even call myself "OK" like they called themselves "Tex." I could just imagine Roy Acuff introducing me at the *Grand Ole Opry*, which I had listened to since 1939. "Here's a new singer called OK Childress," he would say. "Let's give him a big *Opry* welcome!" Then the audience would start to boo. "If we just wanted OK music, we'd listen to the local boys!" they would shout.

It occurred to me that there would be less violence if I wrote the songs instead of singing them. I knew there were certain "givens" in country songwriting. For example, "Givin' you my heart just ain't no good / You bust it plumb apart like a stick of wood" is not a bad test run. You get a simile, and *heart, good, ain't,* and *bust* lend a country flavor. And, of course, *apart, wood,* and *givin'* tug at the emotions, which is what country songwriting is all about. Country songs made no pretense at intellectuality like, say, the music of Frank Sinatra did. They go for the nitty-gritty, as shown in the lines "Drop kick me, Jesus / Through the goal posts of life."

And when I sent it to Acuff-Rose for publication, a secretary there wrote back to say that her uncle's gas station was looking for a man of my talents.

"YOU DAMNED LITTLE WHELPS will never amount to a hill of beans!" an enraged Aunt Sam was shouting, her dentures gripping the stem of her corncob pipe as the stick of stove wood she had just launched whistled past our ears. My brother David and I were in full flight, of course, because even though the right side of her body was withered from polio, Sam could move fast and throw hard with her left arm. If the wood had hit us, it might have done some damage—but on the other hand, what else can you do when a couple of boys have just tied the tails of two of your eleven cats together with binder twine?

So fat and spoiled were those cats, the endeavor probably held little risk, although admittedly, it was a nasty thing to do to a couple of animals that weren't bothering anyone. David had taken a purring cat under each arm, butts forward, while I wrapped the twine around their tails.

"You got to tie 'em tight," he counseled.

"I know it," I said. "Just shut up and hold 'em."

The oblivious, easygoing cats took no action until my little brother dropped them. Then they panicked, clawing at each other to get free. It didn't take them long to slip the tail cuffs, of course, removing some hair (but fortunately, no eyes) in the process, but the noise they made brought Aunt Sam out of her nap and ready for battle. On this rare occasion, her husband—dad's brother Bid, the uncle who used to tell me folksy riddles—was not home. Riding herd on a runty thirteen-year-old and a child of six was asking a lot of anyone, and Sam had special challenges.

Aunt Sam could do things with one arm that many men couldn't do with two. She was a demon for work and never once complained about her life—a life that, for some reason we never understood, included an occasional seizure.

"Look!" David skidded to a stop. "She's havin' a fit!"

I jerked my head around. Aunt Sam was lying on the ground, kicking and frothing at the mouth, her gray head stiffened at an odd angle. The yellow corncob pipe lay in the dirt. It was a frightening sight, and there was nobody around to help. We ran to her, but before we could reach her, she began to revive, raised up groggily, focused on us, and said, "What are you two little devils up to now?" She had completely forgotten our prank.

"You dropped your pipe," I said, feeling ashamed. We helped her up, she took the pipe, and nothing else was said. We never twined her cats again after that.

Bid and Sam Childress were in and out of our childhoods, usually by way of the cotton patch. I stayed with them a couple of times. Aunt Sam could pull bolls so fast with her strong left hand that it was a blur. Meanwhile, she'd be singing a tuneless ditty that sounded like *"¡Boma stela casa poco timbo!"* There were other phrases, but that's the only one I recall. Later, I realized she was trying to say, in her limited Spanish, *"¡Vamos a la casa poco tiempo!"* or "Get to the house right now!"

Sam was an amazing woman in many respects, but she never learned how to make good biscuits. Hers were lumpy, with flour on the outside, and they tasted like bicarbonate of soda. Mom's biscuits were always good, but Sam's made us gag, so we sneaked them to the cats under the table. Those cats would eat anything but binder twine. I knew Aunt Sam and her corncob pipe for years, off and on, and discovered early on that she couldn't say no to a cat. Any cat, the scruffier the better, was welcome to live with her. Cats came, cats defecated (in any of six sandboxes), cats went, cats died—there were always more cats, which pleased my brother and me about as much as turpentined sugar, a cough remedy of the day as vile as it was useless. We hated having all those felines around, but we were stuck there until our parents, who had taken our sisters with them to Arizona to check out the cotton crop, returned for us.

Aunt Sam's real name was Lily. I don't know where she got the nickname Sam, but everybody who knew her called her that because she didn't like the name Lily. She was always puffing away on her corncob pipe, had gray hair, a craggy, narrow face, and a beaklike nose. Her neck leaned way over to one side. In the mean way that kids have, David and I figured that someone that ugly had to be a witch—but in the interest of personal safety, we kept it to ourselves. In later years, looking back, it seemed to me that Aunt Sam bore a strong resemblance to Pansy Yokum in the old comic strip *Li'l Abner*. Pansy smoked a corncob pipe, too.

TWINING WASN'T the only thing we risked a hiding for. There was something even more rotten—turpentining—that my cousins Jimmy and Johnny did. Though I personally never did it, turpentining was a common practice among farm kids in the 1940s. It's been half a century since I watched Jimmy and Johnny turpentine a cat, a procedure that was supposed to scare off cats from my cousins' barn, where upwards of two dozen hung out.

"They's too many danged cats around here," announced Jimmy one spring day.

His brother Johnny promptly said, "Well then, let's us turpentine some. That'll get rid of 'em."

"What's turpentining?" I asked, all innocence.

"Watch and see," said Johnny, a skinny stalk of a kid with unruly brown hair and a cowlick that not even axle grease could tame. Meanwhile, his bigger brother Jimmy was coaxing one of the barn's many cats to him, at which point he grabbed it and brought it to where Johnny waited with his equipment.

The tools were simple—a fresh corn cob and a bottle of turpentine. As Jimmy knelt on his knees and held the cat against his thigh with its butt forward, Johnny grabbed the hind legs, made two or three swift swipes with the cob across the cat's butt, and then splashed turpentine on the irritated area.

The poor beast was yowling piteously, and I felt a deep sense of shame that my cousins would do such a thing. Of course, the felines always recovered in a few minutes, but they walked in bits and pieces for awhile after that, stopping occasionally to investigate and lick the site and then wobbling on.

Naturally, my idiot cousins were helpless with laughter. Then the adrenalin flow slowed, and Jimmy started feeling some real pain where the cat's claws had dug into his thigh at take-off.

"Sumbitch gouged the hell out of me," he moaned, his face screwed up with pain.

"He got me pretty good, too," Johnny said ruefully, holding up a torn and bleeding hand.

"Well, you wouldn't want it to get infected," I said. "Pour some turpentine on it."

Secretly, I was glad they were feeling pain. Jimmy and Johnny will be surprised if there really is a hell, and they go there when they die, and Satan turns out to be a cat.

A WEEK LATER, dad showed up at Aunt Sam's, driving a different car, a maroon Nash, and the next day we said good-bye to her and Uncle Bid and left for Arizona and more cotton rows. Mom and dad had found work around Eloy and Casa Grande, which were dusty, searing desert burgs in 1946 but are good-sized towns today.

The fields were flat, irrigated, and seemed to run forever. The sun was terribly hot, creating shimmering heat waves that distorted the miles of rows and made the acrid smell of cotton hang thick in the air. I hated the work and that smell with all my heart, but I was a good cotton picker, considering my runty size, sometimes even outpicking dad. My brother David, when he got some size on him, was even better. Our family would pick cotton around Eloy and Casa Grande several times in years to come.

The strange thing about leaving Aunt Sam was that my brother and I both missed her almost immediately. Without realizing it, we had grown to love her. We always knew what to expect from her, and she never let us down. The last time I saw her was in 1959, and she was very old. I was home from the military, and I could tell that she didn't have many more years to live. She died three years later, following her husband Bid in death.

Thirty years later, remembering her, I wrote a poem that tried to sum up my feelings for a crippled but strong old woman who bravely played the cards life dealt her.

The Sorceress

"Boma stela casa poco timbo,"
my aunt said, and green corn grew
where she placed her withered feet.
Others thought she was just old and crazy

but I knew she was a witch from the start,
and was fascinated by her gift of tongues.
She talked to roots and berries by the hour,
and they sang back to her.

By the barn one summer day,
she fell down and started kicking.
"Another fit," my father grunted,
but I had seen her earlier

communing with spiders, and knew
she was just casting a spell.
That night the sky grew shimmering trees,
and deep voices split the dark.

Cyclones touched down and hundreds died,
but we were safe. "Thank god," my mother said,
little knowing she had a sorceress to thank.
Years went away, and I left for war

with the forces of evil. She gave me an amulet
to keep me from harm, an enchanted diamond
mined from a broken fruit jar.
When I returned,

I found her in a tin shack, thin boned
and tallowy, dying with no one
to admire her magic.
That night, I sat by her as she slept,

her seamed face softened by candle light,
and at midnight ten thousand stately spiders
came down and wrapped her in gauze,
and carried her webbed spirit away.

A LOT OF MY LIFE has been spent with my eyes glued to portholes or
windows. When you belong to a footloose family, there's a chance
you'll be footloose yourself—although my siblings weren't, at least
not as much as I was.

When I look back on those vagabond days, I realize how lucky we were that mom and dad somehow kept us fed and clothed in the late Depression and postwar 1940s, even though we wore clothes passed from cousin to cousin and patched by mom to make them wear longer. We were full-time migrant workers, which was bad enough. Then dad got the "me farmer, you field hand" bug and started raising crops on the shares. This meant a landowner would let him farm a place—usually with poor soil—and we'd share the crop. Dad's ambition increased our labors, but after our skimpy crops were in, we went back to migrant work again.

We roamed the Southwest in our dilapidated pickup, sleeping in it or beside it, sometimes renting a motor court cabin—usually because mom and dad wanted baths. We kids never wanted baths. Baths were something to be avoided with every wile in our bag of tricks. Unfortunately, dad didn't agree. He would just say, "Git yer little butts in that damn tub! I'm payin' a buck a night for this cabin, and we're gonna get our money's worth!"

Once we'd moved into some migrant workers' shack or other, we kids slept on the dirt floor or in the open-topped trailer on pallets made of old quilts—four kids side by side, feet to head. We couldn't fight that way, but we could kick, and we did. David and I had to be careful because the girls were tattletales and would yell, "Daddy! Bill and David are kicking us!" My brother and I, in imminent peril of having our rumps rearranged, would draw our feet clear up under our chins and sleep that way.

At one such shack, there was room for the kids inside, so I had the back of the pickup all to myself. I'd lie there, playing the harmonica Uncle Guy Childress had given me, which I treasured as the first harmonica I ever had. Years later, I started playing it and my Gibson guitar together, and the next thing I knew some guy named Bob Dylan was imitating me.

"Bill!" dad would finally yell. "Put that French harp up and get some sleep! You'll need it tomorrow!"

Dad wasn't forced to be a rover, he just liked being one. Sometimes he settled down in a town and worked for a year or two, but then he got the itch to roam again—or (worse) to farm again. Only the plowed dirt of a field, in his case poor dirt, could keep him in one place for long. He farmed until he starved out, then we were off again, God knew where, to pick cotton in Texas or citrus in California. For almost two years, he had worked filling ore cars deep under Arizona, giving his family a blessed break from the fields.

But sooner or later, we came back to the Ozark country to try our hand at sharecropping—again. The truth is, my stepfather wouldn't have known farming if it was a bear trap and he stepped in it. He loved to try, though—which meant his family also got to try. To this day, I get hives if I spend too much time around live-stock, tractors, or especially those stinking cotton fields. Their odor alone gives me headaches.

When you're one of a quartet of kids, you aren't as affected by being poor as grown-ups are. Kids are resilient and seldom get cranky if their bellies are full—not that ours always were. Sure, you want fancy toys, but you learn to make your own, and some of these are almost good enough to kill you.

Take slingshots: I made my own out of a small tree fork, rubber strips, and a trimmed leather shoe-tongue. With such a device, I once zinged a marble off my little brother's head and sent him screeching to dad. That one got me got me a thrashing. Needless to say, dad's primitive parenting taught me a fast lesson. I never used a slingshot on my brother again.

The best slingshot rubber was almost impossible to find, espe-cially after World War II broke out. It was red, the real stuff, from prewar inner tubes. Synthetic wartime tubes were useless because they had no stretch. The most money I ever made as a kid was when I found a red inner tube in an old abandoned tire and cut it into strips for slingshots. My pals wanted some of that rubber so bad that they were happy to offer a fortune—a penny for two bands. By day's end, I had close to forty cents and was contemplating buy-ing a car. Best of all, I had enough of that inner tube tucked away to make slingshots until I was fifty.

As for other entertainment, there was plenty to see when we were road-toading, except, of course, in the desert. Even there, we occasionally saw an old favorite—those little red and white signs planted by the Burma-Shave company. My siblings and I rode in the back of the pickup, and they were sometimes sleeping when the signs appeared. So I'd start yelling, "Wake up, wake up! They's more a-comin'!" Up they'd leap to hear me read the signs as they flashed past, responding with giggles to each one.

> Santa's whiskers
> Need no trimmin'
> He kisses kids
> Not the women
> Burma-Shave

The road was Route 66, it was 1946, and our eventual destination was the cotton fields of Bakersfield, California. War's end brought no prosperity to Okie farmers, so dad sold out, lost his shirt in the process, and headed west across the desert. The color scheme was simple—tan earth and blue sky as far as we could see, with a sun like an acetylene torch blazing down on scrub brush and sand.

Besides overheated or sometimes abandoned cars, by far the most entertaining things we kids saw on Route 66 were the little signs bearing jingles for something we wouldn't need for years—shaving cream.

> See how sister
> Raves and rants
> Must have sat down
> On some ants
> Burma-Shave

My sisters didn't like that one as much as I did, but they warmed pretty good to the next one.

> Brother Billy
> Sure is dumb
> Missed the nail
> And smashed his thumb
> Burma-Shave

The beauty of those little verses was that they didn't give a hoot about punctuation of any sort. Spelling wasn't critically evaluated, either, which suited us fine. Glenda was in the second grade and years later would say that she felt the signs helped her learn to read faster. As for David and Helen, they were still too young to read.

Burma-Shave signs were part of America's highway history for almost forty years. Even long ones, which were rare, were easily—and breezily—assimilated:

> Does your husband
> Misbehave
> Grunt and grumble
> Rant and rave
> Shoot the brute
> Some Burma-Shave

The verse was hard to resist. Anyone who could read was drawn to the carefree rhymes, some of which were awful, but none of which were risque. The jingles were carefully screened by the company, which called itself "Burma-Vita." It was impossible to read just one sign and skip the rest—or read the ending first. As one wag observed, "It's just as hard to read one Burma-Shave sign as it is to eat one salted peanut."

My family picked cotton or cut broomcorn all over the South, and to us kids—who had little enough to begin with—those signs were more fun than a tub of baby ducks.

I read somewhere that Burma-Shave's ingredients came from Burma, and since *vita* is Latin for "life," Burma-Vita apparently meant "life from Burma." How such a motto could possibly mesh with a shaving cream, I never figured out. But like two-lane Route 66, Burma-Shave was doomed by progress. New interstates with wide rights-of-way banned close-up signs, and supercities—what we now call urban sprawl—were immune to such homely art. The ever-rising costs of labor dealt the coup de grace. In 1960, the company saved $200,000 a year by discontinuing Burma-Shave. The signs were taken down and destroyed. Some were given to the Smithsonian, where they now reside.

AS I SAID, we sometimes stayed in dollar-a-night auto courts, which dad complained were overpriced. But to us kids, those plank-floored cabins were the lap of luxury. On the other hand, with their kerosene-wick stoves, they could also be laps of death—firetraps that killed more than one migrant family. But at least we could fix a hot meal, even if it was just biscuits and blue john gravy or pork and beans, our mainstays.

Dad's idea of a diet was whatever he could afford to buy. My siblings and I were raised for years on biscuits, fatback, and blue john gravy—made from skim milk with a vaguely bluish color. Another treat was "redeye gravy," beloved of Southerners, made from the dregs of fried sugar-cured ham with a little water added. In other words, lard juice and salt.

On the road, we worried about how much we could carry, or how far we'd get on recapped synthetic-rubber tires. But blowouts were part of the tradition, along with boiling radiators and running out of gas. In the desert southwest, gasoline stations could be one hundred miles apart. An emergency gas can and a Monkey Grip patch kit always joined a jack, crank, and extra spark plugs in the trailer. A worn canvas tarp, tied down, more or less protected our meager possessions.

Years later, when writing a *Westways* story about Route 66 (which really didn't have many kicks), I wondered how the automotive pioneers in the early 1900s crossed America. It turns out that in 1911, a two-and-a-half-ton Packard truck, carrying all its own fuel and supplies, made it from New York to San Francisco, at a time when "highways" ranged from gullies to quagmires. Now, *those* people were motorists. Eight years later, in 1919, an army caravan did the same. A young lieutenant took careful notes of the dangers and setbacks, recognizing how important good roads were to the national defense. Four decades later, as president, Dwight D. Eisenhower signed the interstate highway act into law.

On the road, a loud explosion always meant that searing heat had claimed a tire. The family stayed with our skimpy household goods to foil thieves while dad hitched a ride to the nearest town to buy a used tire or tube. In those 35-mile-per-hour days, folks were easier about picking up hitchhikers. At that speed, you had time to assess their character.

One day, somewhere in New Mexico, our old Hudson lurched hard and came to a dragging stop. My astonished eyes saw a tire and rim go whirling past, broken from the axle of our trailer. It seemed like a simple retrieval, so dad and I took off at a lope to bring the wheel back. But no matter how thoroughly we combed the desert, for hundreds of yards around, we never did find that tire and rim. It was uncanny. The desert had few shrubs and no trees, yet the wheel had vanished like a mirage at sunset. Dad was still bothered by it many years later. "Damndest thing I ever saw," he said. "We should of been able to find it, but we never did."

J. W. Childress, the author's stepfather, age eight, 1923

The author *(center)*, age ten, with cousin Johnny *(left)* and half brother David, 1943

Left to right, front row: David, Johnny, and Jimmy (Johnny's brother); *back row:* the author, cousin Junior (Ray Childress Jr.), and cousin J. W. Childress, 1944

The author as a jump-ready paratrooper, Fort Campbell, Kentucky, 1955

The author as a member of the Eleventh Airborne Division, Augsburg, Germany, 1956, with his Korean War ribbons

The author and his first wife, Rosie, newlyweds, Fresno, California, 1962

The author with his sons *(left to right)* Jason, David, and Chris, 1977

Left to right: Chris, David, and Jason playing around an old Model T, Anderson, Missouri, 1978

The author and his second wife, Diane, 1980

The town of Anderson, Missouri, population 1,265, 1985

The author with a hound named Rascal and his trailer in the background, 1985

The author and his stepfather, J. W. Childress, 1985

The author *(kneeling)* with his stepfather *(center)*, his mother, Lorraine *(on J. W.'s left)*, and relatives at the Childress farm, 1985

J. W. Childress and friend, Anderson, Missouri, March 1987

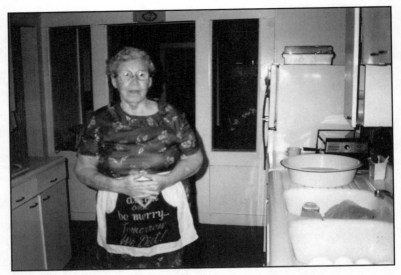

Lorraine Childress in her kitchen, Anderson, Missouri, November 1988

The author *(center)* with his mother and stepfather, Anderson, Missouri, 1990

The author as a regional entertainer, 1992

The author *(center)*
with sons David *(left)*
and Jason and their
mother, Rosie, 2001

William and Diane
Childress, 2004

3

FROM MY WINDOW SEAT, clouds occasionally parted to let me see the Ozarks drifting past below. I'm grateful for the law that bans smoking on airplanes, since the recycled air is bad enough.

"Airborne cattle cars," grumbled my seatmate. "We need a good class-action lawsuit forcing airlines to offer more leg room."

"There's always first class," I said.

As a travel writer, one of my delights has always been the sampling of new foods, new aromas, and new spices. But the more I traveled, the more I began to realize how often people would say, whether they were in Hong Kong or Hungary, that all foreign foods tasted like chicken.

Dining is an occupation fraught with hazards. I can't count the times I've broken a tooth eating pinto beans because someone hadn't picked all the rocks out. But true food lovers don't worry about such dangers. The thought of injury, or even death, from eating some perilous concoction only seems to add spice to new victuals—which may be why the Japanese risk death by eating blowfish. I'm no different. I'll eat anything that doesn't salt and pepper me first.

I once had a friend named Jerry Spumoni who was the ultimate in caloric courage. A photographer and adventurer, he shot leopards in Sri Lanka, polar bears in Canada, and caimans in Brazil. And after he photographed them, he generally ate them. Jerry's diet was as varied as the treasures of the khan. Once he wrote from the wilds of Outer Mongolia, "I went on a tiger hunt yesterday, and today I sampled a native dish that my guide said was made from tiger meat." Jerry explained that the meat in question had been killed in 1905 and preserved by a secret process.

"It's a kind of mud-colored stew," he wrote. "There's nothing like returning to camp after a hunt and devouring a bowl of hundred-year-old tiger stew!" I was eager to find out what it tasted like, so the minute he returned home, I asked him.

"What does hundred-year-old tiger stew taste like?"

He smiled condescendingly. Then he closed his eyes. Anxious moments passed as he struggled for a simile. Finally, he heaved a deep sigh, fixed me with blue, unworried eyes, and said, "It's not easy to describe a dish as exotic as hundred-year-old tiger stew, but I'd say it tastes a lot like chicken."

My late uncle Tom Childress was the victim of one epicurean plot. Told by a fellow in a bar that a gooey mess in a jar was pickled pig's feet, he helped himself. Afterward, his grinning host told him he'd just eaten West Texas rattlesnake. Uncle Tom had couth, I'll give him that. He didn't say a word, just punched the fellow in the mouth and walked out. But Tom's most prevalent hobby had always been tall tales, so the incident gave him new material.

During the Korean War, the army sent me to Eta Jima, the University of the Far East, to study how to blow things up. It was just across the bay from Hiroshima, which the United States had already blown up. We GIs were more interested in Tokyo, anyhow, when we got passes. GIs and Japanese had a love of food in common, the Japanese because World War II wasn't that far behind them, and GIs because the army didn't serve food, only the grim reminders of it. Thus did we fall prey to the slimy octopus, which our Japanese friends felt we should experience.

In Japan, this cephalopod is a universal treat, like popcorn in America. It's eaten raw, smoked, boiled, baked, salt-cured, sake-cured, and for all I know, medically cured. "She's some mighty fine eatin'," said an English-speaking Japanese. "Try her raw. She'll make you remember Japan a long time." She sure would. A description of raw octopus comes hard, but if I said it tasted like rubber bands dipped in Pennzoil, I'd be close.

AS THE PLANE DESCENDED towards St. Louis, I thought how distant the years of my childhood were. Could I possibly be sixty-four? Wasn't I still a fatherless four-year-old with windblown hair, rolling in a clover field for my laughing young mother?

And yet, in my mind's eye I could see my daredevil younger sister, Helen, balancing on a twelve-foot chicken house roof before yelling, "Wonder Woman!" and flying through the air to land shin-deep in a pile of sand. It's a wonder she didn't break her neck. None of us other kids had the nerve. When had that been? Nineteen forty-seven? Helen had been six years old.

As a toddler, my older sister, Glenda, fell into someone's cactus garden and ran screaming to mom, her skin bristling with hair-sized needles. Mom knew it would take forever to pluck them out, so she took a Gillette safety razor and shaved her without lather. The dry blade pulled out the needles. Even if mom didn't know what to do, she did *something*. She never threw up her hands at anything. For all her inner problems, which grew worse as she grew older, mom was durable goods. She was also, at times, a certifiable loony who created many conflicts in her children. We loved her or not, according to, I sometimes thought, the phases of the moon.

I've seen her berating reduce my older sister, then in her fifties, to helpless tears. In a word, the main reason her kids visited so rarely was mom. But as a grandmother, she was in her element, smothering her grandchildren with affection. One day I came upon my middle son, Jason, who was then five. He wore a big smile, and his face was redder than a radish.

"What's so funny, son?" I asked.

"Grandma," he giggled. "She said, 'Gimme sugar!'" *Gimme sugar.* The same phrase that meant "give me a kiss" when I was Jason's age. Some things never change, at least not in the hills.

And there was David, my brother. I could still see him at eight months old, rocking back and forth and crooning in an orange-crate crib in 1940—uttering the same sounds my little granddaughter makes today, the same sounds every child has made since the human race began.

When it came to picture-taking, dad mostly endured it. I've never seen a picture of him when he wasn't standing stiff as a stick, unsmiling and serious. There's one of him in Arizona by a limb-less saguaro, and you can barely tell him from the cactus. Photo-graphs are silent teachers. They tell us we were here, and that our children were here. They sustain us when we grow old, reminding us of the lives we've led. And in most cases, they portray our lives as better than we may have thought they were at the time. Some of those years were horrible, but to a writer, they were pearls of great price. Whatever history is, it isn't dull, and I've always felt that anything a person writes, speaks, or even thinks is some kind of history.

My dad loved the western era. If he can locate Louis L'Amour, Max Brand, or Zane Grey in paradise, he'll kiss their hands. His white Stetson wasn't the only thing "cowboy" about him. He once tried to learn roping. He was awful at it, even after days of prac-tice, but counted it a major victory if he could rope one of our calves for castrating after half a dozen tosses. As for being a rider, he was adequate. At least he never got thrown, which I did. And if he had, he probably wouldn't have landed on a barbed wire fence, which I did. A scar on my left elbow reminds me that Blaze, a sorrel who refused to be broken, taught me to fly in 1949.

One time I was interviewing the oldest citizen of Anderson, Missouri, one hundred and three years old at the time, but dead now for years. I remember saying to him, "Charlie, you must have seen a lot of history in your life."

He was silent for a spell. Then he said, "Seen a lot, fergot a lot."

THE FLIGHT ATTENDANT'S voice cuts into my thoughts. "Something to drink, sir?"

My reverie has made me miss the beverage cart creeping up the aisle. I look up into the tired eyes of a no-longer-young flight at-tendant. A friend of mine was a flight attendant once. She quit after a year, saying the airlines worked them like dogs for low pay—ex-actly the opposite of what passengers believed. It was like being a waitress in a three-hundred-person airborne café. Back in the 1930s

and 1940s, airliners had gourmet food, sleeper berths, and steward-
esses who were registered nurses. Then flying took a giant step
backwards.

"Tomato juice?" I asked.

"Thank you."

A short while later, the captain announced we would be landing in St. Louis in fifteen minutes. From there, I'd catch a puddle-
jumper to Springfield and rent a car. From Springfield, it was still
a hundred miles south to Anderson and another twenty-five miles
to dad's Oklahoma trailer on the shores of Grand Lake. I had caught
a 7:00 AM flight from Sacramento, and with the time changes and
driving, I was hoping to reach Oklahoma before dark.

The plane banks, turning its windows to the sun. Tiny marbles
of light roll across my lap, refractions from the Plexiglas. I'm reminded of some lines from Yeats: *The silver apples of the moon / the
golden apples of the sun.* The flight attendants are back in their small
work area, meaning this part of my journey is ending.

It used to aggravate me that dad, in his entire life, never experi-
enced flying. And when I became a paratrooper, he wrote me off
as completely nuts. I tried everything to get him aloft, ragging him
at every turn, but he wouldn't budge. I knew he was no coward. I
had seen him in action. But there was no doubt at all that he was
as skittish as a new colt when it came to leaving terra firma.

ELOY, ARIZONA, 1947: Late in the afternoon of a sizzling August day,
dad drove his car of the moment down a dusty lane bordered by
cotton to a grower's house. There, he knocked on the door and
stood shuffling his shoes in the sand and telling the owner he had
five pickers available. Four of the pickers waited barefoot in the car,
staring listlessly at a thousand acres of green stalks and white bolls.
There wasn't a tree or a mountain or a river in sight, and the stink
of growing cotton, recently sprayed with DDT, lingered in the air.
Pickers' heads were right down among the leaves and stalks, so
probably I've got some DDT in my system. This was years before
Rachel Carson wrote *Silent Spring*.

The owner and dad walked to the side of the big, white house, where dad shoved his hands into his overalls pockets and chewed on a yellow straw while the grower told him what the wages were (lousy) and what kind of housing was available for migrant families (hovels).

Some cotton camps used surplus army tents, which smelled old, moldy, and tar-soaked in the sun. Never once did we live in anything but the worst kind of shack, often with dirt floors. The government made no inspections, *ever*. Those rich cotton farmers had too much political clout—and too many subsidies. And here is the true division between rich and poor: not so much as a penny of all that taxpayer-generated wealth ever trickled down to migrant workers, then or now. We were the invisible servants of the money gods. To this day, big farmers and ranchers have numerous government programs they can turn to for easy money.

My dad brought us to that world many times over the years. The plight of migrant workers in the 1940s, 1950s, and 1960s was so bad that Edward R. Murrow made a film called *Harvest of Shame*. It's forgotten now, even though migrant workers have it as bad in the twenty-first century as they did in the twentieth. Of course, all this is "just business." Whatever a big farmer can save by cutting corners is profit in his pocket. And a little extra money is enough to make some people a little extra greedy.

Dad really had only three pickers: mom, me, and him. Glenda was eight, and besides being too young, never did become a good picker. David, who would eventually excel at it, was a hard worker, but only seven. Helen, six, played among the rows. As for me, fourteen and a runty ninety pounds, I was expected to pick as much as a grown-up, which meant my hands never stopped flying from dawn to dusk. They grew rough and knobby, and even Noxema helped only a little. Soft hands were a handicap in cotton fields, where thorny burrs gouged like the claws of a cat.

Dad's way of ensuring that I keep a steady pace was to never let me stand up. No matter how much my back ached, if I stood up to relieve it, a green cotton boll the size of a golf ball whizzed past my ear. I wondered how he knew I was standing if his own head was down? He didn't throw to hit me, but occasionally one smacked against me, and it hurt. He never did this where mom could see—but once she caught him and flew into a rage. Right there in the field, with Mexicans, blacks, and Oriental pickers gawking at them, they cussed each other out. What a family! I took my mom's side in that one, though, and many years later, I told dad how much I'd hated those bolls whizzing towards me.

"Aw, hell," he said uncomfortably. "If I hadn't done it, you never would've picked any cotton. Most of the time you just stood up and stared into space."

"That's how a fourteen-year-old runt picked more cotton than a thirty-two-year-old man?" I asked. Dad wisely didn't carry it any further.

"What's done is done. You need to be a little more forgiving." The thought of my cracked and bleeding fingers made me feel more crucified than forgiving. I captured some of those feelings in a sonnet I wrote in the 1960s:

The Weighing Tree

Here, my father said, is another field.
Its stalks were fuller than the ones we'd left
Not many days before, and each would yield
All we might ask of it. Indeed, the drift
Of those white rows of dark clawed burrs of cotton
I can see still, and feel their curving thorns
Piercing my hands. What should have been forgotten
Only recalls the bending, and my brow burns
From the stiff twigs that hid the last low boll.
There was no end to it. My father's goal
Was never mine, and yet I could not see
Beyond the end of rows that had no end,
Except to see the laddered wagon-stand,
And hang my load upon the weighing-tree.

THE DEVIL WORE asbestos in Eloy, Arizona—that's how hot the place got. I once saw a grinning cotton picker showing others how he could fry an egg on the hood of his black car. Sure enough, the edges congealed and turned white, and the yolk slowly baked.

Every morning, we rose in the dark for a meager breakfast of oatmeal or grits and then hit the fields for another fourteen-hour day, sometimes set to music. Tennessee Ernie Ford's "Sixteen Tons" was the tune of one lament:

> Grits in the mornin'
> Black beans at night,
> Corn bread and fry bread
> Rest o' the time.
> How much longer
> Can a cotton picker wait?
> Food's bound to be better
> 'hind the Pearly Gates.

The words drifted over the cotton rows one evening when the air was blue from cooking fires. Pickers moved through the haze like slow-moving ghosts, talking and smoking. The singer and his guitar were out of tune, but there was something hopeful and haunting in the improvised ballad. Finally a harmonica kicked in, and that was when, lying on my pallet in the bed of dad's pickup, I drifted off to sleep.

Dad made us hit the cotton rows early because dew made the bolls weigh heavier, and it was cooler for picking. By 9:00 AM, the sun was a white-hot rivet, and the rest of the day would be worse. We ate salt tablets to replace what we lost in sweat, and mom made us kids wear poke bonnets. No one could get enough water. The fields were made hotter by the humidity from irrigation, and the dark green rows, some still muddy, held an acrid odor that was intensified by being stooped over with your head among the leaves. I still get nauseated thinking about it. There were times in the fields when I got so sick I vomited.

"We'll take a longer break at noon for dinner," dad would say, but he didn't always live up to those promises. It depended on whether he'd just gone into hock for another used car or pickup. If he had, he needed money for payments, and that meant longer hours in the fields for all of us.

Down the half-mile rows we would toil, our canvas sacks trailing like long, white worms. Every so often, like every picker, I'd wrestle my twelve-foot sack onto its bottom, grab the sides, and bounce it to pack the cotton down. A well-tamped sack could weigh a hundred pounds. So solid were they, they bent only a little when pickers wrestled them onto their shoulders to start the trek to the nearest scales. This could be a long trek, but nobody minded. Walking with a twelve-foot canvas sausage balanced on your shoulder was restful when compared to bending among the bolls.

After weighing, we climbed the narrow ladders leaning against the wagons, which were enclosed with chicken wire. Wobbling on the loose piles of cotton, we shook out our sacks, making it last as long as possible to ease our aching backs. This was the only break I got, but if dad thought I was taking too long, he would yell, "Hurry up, Bill! They's others a-waitin'!" That didn't always win him friends. Plenty of folks were in no hurry at all to shake out and get back to the rows. As for dad, he never did anything in a hurry. Mom once called him "the slowest thing on two legs."

One day in an Eloy field, I was bent way over, arms swinging in the rhythm that made the bolls fly into my sack. It was good, thick, short-staple cotton, easier to pick than the long-staple stuff, and I had long since discovered a way to put myself into a kind of trance so the day would pass faster.

Trance or not, I became aware of a buzzing in my ears, a dry, whispery sound that I wanted to go away so I could keep my rhythm. Irritated, I attacked the stalks more vigorously. The buzzing increased, grew in tempo and rhythm. It was practically in my face now.

"*Wa-a-a-u-g-h!*"

Two tiny obsidian eyes, a twitching tail, a dusty body, and a forked tongue spelled *get-the-hell-away* better than any dictionary. To this day, I don't know how I did it, because I was strapped to a fully packed twelve-foot sack of cotton. But somehow, my ninety-pound body leaped up and back with enough strength to double the sack over itself and land me on my butt in the dirt. Such is the power of adrenalin. I scrambled to my feet, glad I hadn't crapped in my overalls.

The snake was no more than a ruler's length from my face. "Rattler!" I yelled. "They's a danged *rattlesnake* over here!"

Ecology hadn't been invented yet, and even if it had been, there were too many little kids playing among the stalks for us to worry about one snake. Men came rushing from all directions, and soon they were displaying a good-sized rattler minus his rattles, which someone had pocketed to use as a watch-chain charm. With doctors few and far between, and with antivenin nonexistent in a scruffy little burg like Eloy, the men did what they had to do. There was no shortage of rattlesnakes, which usually fled the noise of pickers coming down the rows. This one had chosen to protect its turf. Had I been bitten, I would almost certainly have died, for it was the extremely venomous Mojave Green, which can kill as quickly as a cobra.

OUTSIDE EL PASO, TEXAS, in September 1949, the night was bitterly cold, and my teeth were clicking like spoons in a hillbilly band. Clad only in a chambray shirt and Levi's, I was freezing. Damnation Texas! How could it be boiler-room hot in the daytime and bone-biting cold at night? The answer lay in the 6,500-foot altitude I found myself at. Years later, I would hear a line from a song that perfectly fit my image of the state I picked so much cotton in: "Happiness is looking at Texas / in my rearview mirror!"

My situation wasn't helped by the fact that I was hunched and shivering inside a steel culvert—the only shelter I could find after a rancher dropped me off in the high desert. "Sorry, kid," he said. "My ranch is way out yonder, and I can't take you any further. El Paso ain't very far, and you'll probably get a ride before you know it."

It was warm when he dropped me off, but I never got a ride,

and once the sun was gone, the high-plains cold set in. I walked, shivering like a strummed string, thinking about dad in his box-car days, the same age I was now, shaking like this. He was in his seventies before he told me about trying to gather enough news-papers to insulate himself—finding in the process that newspapers made lousy blankets.

Lights glittered in the distance like icicles on an evening barn, but I knew better than to walk a highway at night. It's a good way to become road sausage. So I crawled into the next culvert I saw, teeth chattering and bones aching, too cold to sleep even if the steel ridges let me. I stayed awake all night except for fitful catnaps, occasion-ally vacating the culvert to jump around outside until my blood cir-culated again. A coyote's howl drew a lonely spiral against the night. I was ending my first day on the road, after running away from a cotton field near Lamesa where the family was picking—and right now, I was regretting it, cotton patch or no cotton patch. I was never so glad to see anything in my life as I was to see the sun come up.

Years later, when my middle son, Jason, said he was going to run away from his home in California, where he also lived with a step-father, I wrote him about my own adventure. I don't know if it did him any good, but at least he didn't run away.

I hadn't a clue as to what I might encounter on the road, but my dad knew. He called the Texas Rangers. However, by the time that overhyped agency located me, I was already in jail in Tucson. For my own protection, of course. The official charge was vagrancy.

Uncle Ray, a short, brown-haired, quick-tempered man, drove 125 miles from Miami to Tucson—about three hours in 1949—to pick me up. He was hopping mad. He knew only one way to act with wayward kids, and that was vitriolic. Signing me out, he snarled, "Now, by God, you'll stay with me until your daddy can arrange to ship you home! You try anything with me, and you'll be damn sorry." Being a teenager, I never realized I had cost him a day off work. I only knew his words made me reflect on how I'd gotten there—and why I had no intention of staying.

THE DAY BEFORE I ran away from that Texas field, I stood up in my row, my mind in turmoil. (*Whizzz* came a cotton boll). I was sick to death of cotton fields, cutting broomcorn, picking melons, all the stoop labor *Norteamericanos* loathe and leave to minorities or to the poor, who harvest the melons for their plates, the oranges for their tables. I had to escape, but where to?

After awhile, the thought came to me that I could go to California and become a jockey. I had the runty body necessary for it. I gave no thought to how I'd get there. I was fifteen, weighed less than a hundred pounds, and still had little schooling.

Our overall lot got worse and worse under dad's poor management. True to his patriarchal ways, he handled all the family affairs—badly. At this time, the shack we lived in was a twelve-by-twelve-foot room with a swept-dirt floor and hot and cold running rats. Cockroaches added their charms in spite of mom's ongoing attempts to keep the dump clean.

Mom saw dad's financial flops as the mirror of the man, used them as fuel for her rages, and vented aplenty when she and dad clashed. All of these things worked against me, plunging me into a bottomless pit of despair. Enough was enough. I hit the road as my father had before me, but I chose the highway instead of the freight yards.

While the others ate Sunday breakfast in the dirt-floored hovel the farmer allowed his cotton pickers, I went out through the fields towards the highway and squatted down, thinking.

I scrawled my name in the sand at the end of a cotton row with a twig. Then I threw the twig down, and with heart pounding, walked out to the highway. In a matter of minutes, I was sitting next to a trucker. Fifty miles later, he let me out, and shortly afterward a salesman picked me up, a nice guy who questioned me about being so small and on the road.

"I'm nearly sixteen," I said defensively. He looked astonished.

"I'd have taken you for ten," he said. "Anyway, I think you should go back home." I said I couldn't and rode with him for five hours, at which time he gave me a dollar and a pair of almost new Levi's—

miles too big—to take the place of the patched and faded overalls that was my field garb. "Good luck, kid," he said.

I LEFT UNCLE RAY'S the moment I could sneak away. I remember seeing his old black car coming, searching for me, as I trudged up a hill towards Globe. Realizing he hadn't seen me, I ducked below the bank and watched his angry face drive past. Poor Ray. He and his alcoholic wife were divorced, and all his children but one were gone. His own life was not such as to make him a sweet-tempered man.

I got as far as Deming, New Mexico, before a cop saw me in a local drugstore, baggy Levi's and all, eating a cheeseburger whose twenty-five-cent price tag just about ruined my fifty-cent fortune.

"What you doin' here, son?" he asked.

"Eating."

"Well, I got a place where the food's free. Come on out and get in the car."

Two days and nights in the Deming jail, with gluey oatmeal as the free food, made me want out real bad. At 7:00 AM on a Sunday morning, they finally turned me loose on my word that I would go straight home and gave me a Peter Paul's Almond Joy to speed me on my way. Lamesa was maybe 350 miles from Deming. A trucker took me to Hobbs, New Mexico, and a farmer carried me on to Lamesa. I walked into the shack just as the family was sitting down to eat supper.

"I'm back," I said.

Glenda, David, and Helen stared at me, and mom did too. Dad was silent, not even looking at me. Just as he did years later, after I came home from the Korean War, he pretended nothing momentous had happened in his stepson's life.

"Better sit down and eat," mom said finally. "I expect you're hungry."

Wolves are hungry. I was ravenous. And when I saw my favorite dish—pinto beans with hamburger chunks in them—I ate until I almost busted. Dad never did mention my hobo-style journey. The way he acted, I might never have left. But he didn't throw cotton balls at me after that, and as for my running away, I think he saw himself in my desperation to escape the miseries of migrant life.

We left Lamesa and returned to more sharecropping in Oklahoma, and never again would we do field work as a family in any fields but our own. I turned sixteen and then seventeen. Four months and twenty days after my birthday, North Korea invaded South Korea, and the United States was back at war.

"Jesus Christ," dad muttered. "We're barely out of World War II."

WHILE I STILL DID my share, dad and I both knew something was gone from the old order. I was still small-framed and short, but now I acted more independent, and he treated me like more of an equal.

In his direct way, the way of all the fathers he had ever known or emulated, he felt he was doing the right things to make me a man. Life was hard. There was pain, disappointment, and despair. A man's job, if not his fate, was to endure and fight back if he could. Dad never in his entire life said, "I love you," and he sure never taught me to say it. I learned on my own, and I did tell my kids that I loved them, which didn't stop the pain I caused them. Dad taught me how to plow, plant, work hard at whatever I did, and take it on the chin. Mostly, that's what I have done, and I never could have done so without him.

On my eighteenth birthday, he drove me to Lawton and the Greyhound station. We were both silent during the ride. Dad was losing a field hand, but he'd also have one less mouth to feed. I wanted my freedom, so it was a win-win situation.

A bus took me to Oklahoma City and to the recruiting office where I enlisted in the army. Or tried to. The enlistment sergeant saw my diminutive size and refused to believe I was eighteen. I had no birth certificate, only my stepfather's affidavit.

"Tell you what, kid," he said, as I saw my hopes of escaping from the farm fading. "At a hundred and three, you're two pounds under the army's weight limit. I can tell you really want in, so go drink plenty of water and eat a lot of bananas, and come back. Maybe we can get you by."

I haven't exactly loved bananas since, but it worked. I'll always be grateful to that recruiter, because for all the military's crap (right in there with corporate crap), joining the army was the best thing I could have hoped for. In my seven years as a combat engineer in the Korean War and then as a paratrooper, I matured beyond my wildest dreams. The runt who ate bananas to pass the weight requirement got out of the army weighing a hundred and sixty five pounds and hard as a rock.

I was in a daze of excitement through the first two weeks, and then I was sent to Fort Jackson, South Carolina, for basic training. In March 1951, I was the smallest man in the Thirty-first Infantry Division. Someone took a picture of me standing next to the biggest man and labeled it "Mutt & Jeff." A number of bad things happened during my time there, and I grew to despise the deep South and what it stood for in those days—rampant ignorance, racism, and Bible-banging. I was very glad when I entrained for a desert army base called Fort Huachuca, Arizona, for advanced training. It was early 1951, and the body count in Korea was rising.

When we trainees arrived at Fort Huachuca one night in April 1951, we were screamed off the train by noncoms and jogged a mile to our barracks—like we needed that to make us tired. We were already exhausted after a three-day ride from South Carolina. That night I fell asleep unaware that I would soon meet a nasty little critter with its tail cocked like a trigger. A scorpion moved into my boot, and the next morning I moved out of it, yelling like a banshee. As an Ozark farm boy, I had rarely seen a scorpion, much less felt one. Damn but it hurt! Some of the guys thought the incident was funny, but I had the last laugh. My swollen foot meant no drill for three days.

The Korean War now occupied all our thoughts. We were here to become combat engineers, training in what somebody had called "the army's biggest sandbox." World War II was only six years behind us, and our equipment was from that war, including the old strap-type combat boots—choice of discerning scorpions everywhere. But basic equipment was secondary; our mission was to become engineers, and our training emphasized that. Naturally, they couldn't fit anyone as small as me with fatigues, so my uniforms were very baggy. One sergeant said, "Childress, you look like a duffel bag."

At the end of my first week, I wrote a letter to my folks. In those days, the army worried about such things and ordered us to write home. I would have in any case, although my folks rarely wrote back. Here is one mom saved for many years and gave back to me before she died.

APRIL 10, 1951

FORT HUACHUCA, ARIZONA

Dear Mom, Dad, Glenda, David, and Helen:

I am at Fort Huachuca, which means "wind" in Apache, where I am training for the Korean War as a Combat Engineer. I looked at a map and found out that Eloy is only 100 miles away, just to give you an idea how hot it gets here. I was stung by a scorpion a week ago but am now fine. This place is a lot of sand and low brush but the Huachuca Mountains are visible. Our training is partly putting together Bailey Bridges, kind of like a big erector set, and pontoon bridges, with a lot of training in the use of explosives. There is a new one called Composition C-3 that you can shape like biscuit dough. I am MOS 3533, Demolitions Specialist, which pays a hazardous duty bonus of $55 a month. I only make $52 a month, so that will really help.

Well, my arms are sore from shots and tomorrow comes early—reveille is at 5 AM. I'll write you all again soon.

Love, Bill

THE ARMY WASTED no time in living up to its reputation of fitting square pegs into round holes. Korea is a cold, mountainous country, so it followed that we would train on flat, scorching desert. Our barracks, built in World War II, stood bleached and forbidding, but at least they were air-conditioned—every time the wind blew through them.

After we settled in and had our haircuts reaffirmed, we headed for the mess hall. About the only thing I had liked about South Carolina was hominy grits, a staple in the South. I'd eaten them in Oklahoma, too, and naturally assumed any civilized place would have them. So when I didn't see any, I asked.

"Got any grits?"

The PFC serving the fried potatoes gave me a blank look, but the head cook, a staff sergeant, heard and came over. He asked me to repeat myself.

"I was just asking about the grits," I said.

"Grits?" The sergeant frowned. Then a smile lit his features. "Oh, *grits*," he said. "Sorry, soldier, it's B Company's turn to serve grits. Just take your tray with you and cut across the parade ground. They don't mind a breakfast guest now and then."

I reflected on how kind and sincere he was, thanked him, and headed for B Company's mess hall. But once there, after waiting in their chow line a very long time (regulars ate before guests), I was told by another head cook that Sergeant Bull—for that was his name—had it wrong.

"Only C Company serves grits on Wednesdays," he said. "He ought to have known that. They'll fix you up, though."

"Where's C Company?"

"Over by A Company," the cook grinned. "Where you just come from."

Back I trudged, carrying the shiny steel tray. There, another mess sergeant explained that I had been misinformed; it was D Company's turn to cook grits today. So away I went, although by now, chow time was almost over. Halfway there, I heard a shout and looked up to see the first sergeant marching towards me.

"Private," he said, "I've been watching you. What are you doing with that mess tray, walking back and forth across the drill field?"

I explained about the grits. When I was through, he said, almost tenderly, "Son, there ain't a grit in Arizona unless you count a billion tons of sand. That's because grits is a Southern dish, and I ought to know 'cause I'm from Alabama. Those cooks are pulling your leg. Now, you better get on back or you'll miss breakfast entirely." He hadn't so much as smiled during his lecture, but when I stole a look back as I marched, he was hanging onto a corner of the reviewing stand and shaking like a man with malaria.

WE TRAINED in the hottest temperatures I'd ever seen, but the air was dry, so I didn't notice it like I had in the South, which oozes humidity. I was now taking demolitions training, handling real explosives with a calmness I did not feel. But eventually, training took over, and I became one of the coolest powder monkeys anyone could ask for. In time, I would be shipped out to Korea to ply my trade blasting down cliffs to make gravel for runways.

By this time, I'd made a staunch friend, a little New York Jew named Jobe, who was actually smaller than I was. Regular meals and exercise had put some pounds on me, and I now weighed a whopping one hundred and twenty pounds—a little less after hours of sweating during Bailey bridge construction.

I tried to explain Southern cooking to Jobe, and he tried clueing me in to Jewish food. Neither of us had much success. I could barely say *gefilte fish*, much less know what it tasted like—not that it was available, either in the mess hall or in the scraggly civilian settlement outside the main gate. During our limited free time, Jobe and I rented horses and rode around the fort's seventy-three thousand acres. It was a historic place, as we found out when we explored its origins in the post library.

"The *library?*" our disbelieving buddies would exclaim. "What can you do *there?*"

But Jobe and I both loved reading and discovered things that allowed us to be semi-expert in certain fields, should anyone ask. The question most often asked by the eighteen-year-old trainees was, "Anybody going to the beer hall?" It was a new thing, being able to get drunk at eighteen, wobble back to the barracks, and cruise the dizzy skies on an army bunk until you were forced to the latrine to vomit.

Jobe and I learned that Fort Huachuca was built in 1877 to combat outlaws and Indians and was the oldest surviving U.S. cavalry post. From here, "Black Jack" Pershing had pursued Pancho Villa while commanding his Negro cavalrymen, which gave him his nickname. They were called "buffalo soldiers" by the Indians, who compared their hair to that on a buffalo's hump. Pershing never caught Pancho Villa, and no wonder: His army was visible for miles. It even included an airplane!

A famous colored American, Joe Louis, was stationed at Fort Huachuca during World War II, when it was an all-Negro army base. He built The Green Top, a large wooden bar and dance hall outside the main gate, so the soldiers would have some place to go. It may be gone now, but it was still there in 1992, when I last visited the fort. It was off-limits to us trainees in 1951, though.

It was there that I made history as an orator, sort of, shortly before we finished our training. Since we were all under twenty-one, we had to drink beer at the beer-X on base. Now, the only thing more tantalizing than forbidden fruit is forbidden beer. The Green Top was forbidden, so one night, several of us, including Jobe, decided to go there and toast our upcoming journey to Korea.

We drank two beers and were seriously eyeing a third when a pair of large MPs joined the party.

"You guys twenty-one?" a beefy corporal asked.

Well, of course, we weren't, and, of course, they herded us outside. They were getting ready to load us into a three-quarter-ton truck when I stepped up to the corporal (all five feet three inches of me) and said, "You know, Corporal, what you're doing is a damned shame! Every one of us is boarding a ship for Korea in four weeks, and chances are we'll be dead in six months!" This wasn't exactly kidding; Harry Truman's War hadn't gone well and had claimed a lot of American lives.

"I ask you, Corporal, what is our crime? What have we done that deserves a court-martial and maybe the stockade? Did we hurt anyone? Start any trouble? No, we did not! We just wanted to drink a beer in a civilian place after weeks of hard training, before they ship us out to our deaths! I guess it all boils down to this, Corporal. We're old enough to get our brains blown out in a war, but we're too young to drink a beer in Joe Louis's bar!"

The MPs stared at me. Then they looked at each other. Finally, the big corporal, hiding a smile, said, "Go on, get outta here, but we better not see you here again."

Jobe said later it was one of the finest speeches for personal liberty he'd ever heard.

He was dead within a week.

SOMEWHERE, I STILL HAVE a picture of my little Jewish friend, squinting into the desert sun. If he were alive, he'd be over seventy now, like me.

We were getting ready to load into trucks and return from the demolitions range where we'd been learning about the versatility of primer cord by cutting down small desert trees. You wrapped the cord around the trunk at whatever level and set it off. It operated like a flexible blasting cap to cut the tree in two.

One day as we headed back to the base five miles away, the two-and-a-half-ton truck carrying Jobe's demolition squad took a curve too fast, turned over, and rolled down an embankment. It landed on top of the soldiers. I was in a jeep just behind and watched it happen in disbelief—the truck becoming top-heavy, the huge wheels slowly lifting on one side, a terrible cloud of dust, ripping canvas, and snapping wooden struts, followed by silence. The first sounds to break that dreadful quiet were the screams of men pinned under the splintered wreckage.

Much had happened in my life since I turned eighteen. Now death was added to the mix, the death of a friend. Seeing those men, the dust of the desert mixed with their blood, their broken bones poking through flesh like the shattered wooden arcs poking through canvas, hearing the screams and groans—it all put me in a kind of shell shock.

It took twenty men and two jeep winches to raise the truck. Jobe was taken to surgery, but his skull had been crushed, and he was doomed. I was standing with others in the dispensary when a lieutenant came out and said, "He's gone." Jobe was the only one to die, but two others were so badly mangled they were sent home to a lifetime of disability.

There would be little time to mourn. In a few weeks, I'd be in Camp Stoneman, California, where I'd board the USS *Marine Serpent,* a seasick-making, round-bottomed Liberty ship for Pusan, Korea. First, though, I had a fifteen-day furlough coming.

MY FOLKS HAD NO PHONE—there were no rural phones around there—so when the Trailways bus dropped me in Chickasha, a scrawny little farming town of perhaps one thousand people (closer to twenty thousand today), I slung my duffel bag over my shoulder and started walking. It was May 1952, sunny and warm, and I was wearing my summer khakis—although now they fit better because I had grown both up and out.

I didn't have to walk far before a gray-stubbled old farmer in a clatter-de-bang pickup stopped. Tossing my duffel in the back, I climbed up front with him. He smelled of sweat and tobacco.

"You say your dad is Jay Childress?" he asked, after I'd given him a little history. "Sure, I know him. Farms the old Coldwell place a mile from mine. He ain't had a lot o' luck, though—but then, the Coldwell place ain't one of the best farms a feller might lease."

What else was new? I sometimes felt that the owners of the very worst places saw dad coming and rubbed their hands together with glee. The farmer let me out by our mailbox. From there, a rutted clay driveway led to a shacky-looking bungalow with two chinaberry trees out front. Not far away slumped a chicken house that had probably been built during the Oklahoma land rush. But a garden between the house and the poultry fence was coming along nicely, with green corn and tomatoes brightening the area.

The garden was about all that looked good. Dad had leased another loser, seedy and run down. The "corrals" were interwoven blackjack limbs, crude and not very effective. Inside them was stapled a hog-wire fence to imprison the dozen or so grunting pigs he had. There were chickens, cows in a nearby pasture, a pair of mules, and a beat-up old Oliver tractor—the kind with a single front wheel.

My little brother David saw me first. He stared at the khaki apparition trudging down the driveway with a shouldered duffel and raced into the house, yelling at the top of his lungs, *"It's Bill! It's Bill!"* He was now eleven, a towheaded stalk of a kid who was quickly joined by his sisters. God, they were all growing up. I saw dad, a pail of feed in his hand, poke his head out of the barn at the commotion. Then he started towards the house—slowly, of course. Mom came down the steps, grinning broadly as she took in her soldier son. Both of them looked older than they should. Dad was thirty-seven, mom thirty-nine.

"You've growed," she said in amazement—for she had long believed I never would reach "normal" height.

"Well, some," I admitted. "I'm five feet four now, and I weigh one twenty-five."

"That's *lots* more than you did when you enlisted," mom beamed, hugging me, "and a whole inch higher!" (I would eventually gain forty-five pounds and four inches more in height, thanks to the army.)

Inside, the past came back with a vengeance. In spite of all mom could do to make it a home, this forlorn edifice had no wallpaper, no linoleum on the floor, and no indoor plumbing—which I'd gotten used to in the army. I took my first shower and owned my first toothbrush in the army. All baths we kids took at home were in shared bath water in a galvanized washtub. We just added more homemade lye soap. What germs could live through that? As for our teeth, we chewed twigs until the end made a "brush" and then used that with a salt-and-soda mixture. Only now, as I sit in a comfortable home with all the amenities, can I comprehend how amazingly poor we were—so poor that the army seemed luxurious to me. Best of all, I had my own bed. At home, I'd had to share with my little brother David, who usually peed on us during the night.

A potbellied cast-iron heater sat in the middle of the living room, and an old range occupied a corner of the kitchen. The heater, mom said, was new, but everything else looked worn-out and tired, and to tell the truth, so did dad and mom. The kids looked okay. They were enrolled in school, bused by an old wood-sided yellow school bus, and somehow I knew their field-work days were over, too. The family was tired of the sharecrop/migrant worker cycle that had sapped their lives, and changes were coming.

Dad looked like a stranger. Never an emotional man, his expression didn't change when he saw me in uniform. We shook hands, and he said, "Come on out to the barn with me while ma gets supper ready. Got something to show you."

I did. In the center aisle, shining in the unlit gloom, was a brand-new-used Nash. "Three years old," dad said proudly. "I got a hell of a deal on it."

FOR THE FIRST COUPLE of days, my siblings followed me around like I was some attractive stranger, and I basked in it. They asked me about the army, and I lied as much as I could, so that by the time the topic was exhausted, they were ready to enlist themselves.

"You get to shoot real guns?" David asked.

"Big ones," I said. "M-1 rifles, and they kick like a mule."

I grinned as a memory came back. "Dave, remember the time I let you shoot that old .20-gauge of dad's? The one he killed the skunk with?"

David frowned. "'Course I do," he said. "You had me shoot it in a squatting position so it would knock me down!"

"Well, maybe it'll make you feel better to know that an army rifle kicks even harder than that," I said.

"Durn!" he said. "I wish I could shoot one!"

But eventually David would change his mind. He would go through his life without ever entering military service. So would Glenda and Helen. By the time I was finally out of the military, seven years later, they had all grown up and married. I had chosen a more adventurous path—training to be a demolitions specialist, fighting a war, becoming a paratrooper, and going to college, all the way to a Master of Fine Arts degree. In that whole family, I was the only one to ever go to college, much less be a writer.

My sisters wanted to know if there were women in the army, and I said, "Sure. We've got WACs. We have colored soldiers, too."

"Colored soldiers?" asked dad.

"Right in with the whites."

"Well, ain't that a pretty picture," he growled. "But I suppose they ain't much good as soldiers?"

"They're some of the best," I answered, knowing my dad would never believe it. "One was a hero during hand-grenade practice. A trainee dropped a live grenade in his pit—the permanent foxholes we throw from—and this colored private grabbed it, threw it out of the pit, and pulled the other soldier down just as it exploded. He got a medal for it."

Dad said nothing after that. Like so many Republican hawks who evaded Viet Nam, including George Bush, his own military service held no shining hours. One year after enlisting in 1933, he had bought his way out.

WHEN IT CAME TIME for me to go back to Fort Huachuca, I hugged mom and told the kids good-bye as they left for school. Everybody knew I was going to Korea, but there wasn't a lot they could do about it. Mom's hug seemed tighter than usual. Dad drove me to the Chickasha bus station, and we shook hands. Then he said, "Well, so long," and was back in the car and gone. No shoulder slap, no "proud of you, son," no emotion at all, even though I was headed for war. *Build the wall, put up a barrier between yourself and anything that might cause pain.*

I was a man now, dad's style, and such emotional stuff wasn't necessary. Maybe he wanted to make sure I was finally out of the den, a young wolf ready to make his way or die in the process. Maybe he never thought of it quite that way, but he knew that I was definitely on my own.

When I was finally in Korea, my first letter from mom told me that the day dad returned from the bus station, he said, "Let's leave this place." She agreed, and after a quick farm sale, they headed west again. This time, they stayed in California fifteen years before returning to the Ozarks, to their last farm, and to their final resting place.

IN SEPTEMBER 1952, we left Camp Stoneman early on a hazy morning to board a World War II Liberty ship, the USS *Marine Serpent*. As we steamed under the Golden Gate Bridge and the squat, gray walls of Alcatraz fell behind us, the dreaded prison seemed to sink into the water, an illusion, but real enough to fix it indelibly in my mind. The image gave rise to "Korea Bound, 1952," one of my most anthologized poems.

> Braced against the rise and fall of ocean,
> holding the rail, we listen to the shrill
> complaining of the waves against the hull,
> and see the Golden Gate rise with our motion.
> Some hours previous, bearing duffels
> as heavy as our thoughts, we wound inward
> like slaves in some gigantic pyramid,
> selected by our Pharaoh for burial
> against our wills. Now we watch Alcatraz
> sink into the water, and visualize
> the pale, amorphous masks of prisoners,
> whose lack of freedom guarantees their lives.

Those round-bottomed old boats could be relied on to wallow like bathing elephants, creating some of the finest seasickness any GI ever suffered. Even the sailors got sick sometimes, so imagine us landlubbers when we really got out to sea. So many of us were lined up along the rails, vomiting over the sides, it looked like a picket fence. Occasionally the wind from the bow would whip someone's spew back into our faces, and that would start the agony all over again. Most of us were certain we'd die on the ship, so we didn't worry about dying in any war.

There were days of seasickness and weeks of boredom before we docked in the dirty harbor of Pusan, where I was put on a train headed north. As it turned out, I would be the only soldier let off at Pyongtaek, my destination—now little more than stalks of concrete from previous battles. Already the armies had see-sawed up and down the peninsula from Pusan to the Yalu River and back, and guerrilla groups were doing their part, blowing up bridges and tracks.

The Chinese had entered the war a year earlier, and Russian MIGs were flying against us—yet amazingly, no world war had been started. Truman had fired the megalomaniac MacArthur, or there probably would have been one. No soldiers I ever knew were admirers of Dugout Doug, the PR Machine. He'd been born and bred in the Arkansas Ozarks, right down to his oversized corncob pipe. But nothing could have been more oversized than Mac's ego.

As the train chuffed northward, the weather turned rainy and cold. When it shuddered to a halt where Pyongtaek had been, I jumped off and looked around at the flat rice paddies, wrinkling my nose at the odor of human feces used as fertilizer. (Today, Pyongtaek is a city of more than 250,000.)

I leaned my duffel against what had once been a square column in a railroad station. A jeep was supposed to meet me, but there was no jeep in sight. A bullet-gray sky and a crumpled moonscape, muddy and devoid of human life, were all I saw of a former village. Pyongtaek was situated south of Seoul, on the muddy shores of the Yellow Sea. The paddies around it had once sprouted rice, but now a new two-mile runway would sprout in their stead.

In a puddle by my boot, I noticed a bent stick. Idly, I toed it— and five tiny fingers suddenly flipped up from the water. I recoiled in horror. The stick was the arm of someone's child. Farm kids are no strangers to death, but this hit me hard—a toddler's hand and arm lying in a shallow crater. Where was the rest of the body? I realized that I didn't want to know—that indeed, my mind was already closing mental hatches.

I had seen dead cows and hogs on the farm, but these were human remains. The realization hit home that violent battles had been fought here, and this poor child, who could have been anyone's baby, was killed in one. An artilleryman who couldn't see what he fired at had sent an artillery shell skirling to where the child stood, and those who fired it never knew a toddler had been blown to pieces. In peacetime, had they done the same thing, they might have been put to death. Murder in war only carries death penalties for the innocent. I thought of my sisters and brother back home. It was only the luck of the draw that part of them wasn't lying in that muddy crater.

Where the hell was that jeep?

Finally it skidded into sight, slewing back and forth on the muddy road, its engine whining. A corporal braked to a stop and got out, a tall, skinny galoot with unruly red hair poking out from under his helmet liner.

"You PFC Childress?"

"Yes, Corporal."

"Let's go."

I tossed my duffel in the back, and on the way to the base, I mentioned what I'd seen. He shrugged. "You see things like that from time to time. Dogs dig 'em up, or rain washes 'em up. They had hellish battles around here early last year—the whole damn North Korean army pushed our guys almost to Pusan. My brother was in on that. He said most of his buddies had their ship picked out to go home on. Then the tide turned, and they drove the gooks back."

The jeep's brakes squealed, and we slithered to a halt. "Whoa!" the corporal said. "How the hell did I miss *him*?" A dark, half-submerged lump floated in a paddy ditch. A young soldier of the R.O.K. (Republic of South Korea) about my age, one rigid arm curving up out of the water, lay before us. Closer inspection revealed a small hole in his breastbone.

The corporal looked around nervously. "Could of been a damn sniper," he said. "We'll report it to the Graves Registration people. They'll pick him up and give him to the R.O.K.'s. That's all we can do." We drove on to the bivouac area.

I ONCE HAD a photograph, faded and creased, that showed me grinning ferociously into some soldier's clicking glass eye. Oversized field trousers oozed down my one-hundred-twenty-pound frame, my boots were smeared with Korea's yellow mud, and both my hands held blocks of TNT. My blond hair was crew cut and spiky in Korea's October sun, and the terrain around me was flat farm-land, dotted with Koreans busy at a grim task—the relocation of centuries of their dead. War is no respecter of religion. It just uses religion for its own purposes.

The cemetery's acres would soon be an airstrip for U.S. Saberjets, Skyraiders, and the prop-driven P-51 Mustangs of the R.O.K. Air Force, whose pilots hot-rodded the fast little planes to beat all hell. The air was cold. Winter was coming fast. But the smell of rotting human bodies cramped my nose and surely seeped through the white masks worn by the removal crews. Despite that, I felt a sense of awe, of strangeness, and even a kind of excitement that only a nineteen-year-old farm kid seven thousand miles from home could feel. President Truman's "police action" had been my ticket off that farm, my escape from the migrant trail, and to someone used to following farting mules down furrows, human bodies, some of them centuries old, weren't especially daunting.

The airstrip was being built in a long, narrow valley near the shores of the Yellow Sea—not far from where MacArthur made his much-hyped Inchon landing. All around me were huge earthmoving machines—D-8 Cats, Mississippi Mud Wagons, and countless dump trucks, all of them a drab green. Most were in motion, and the long, wavering lines of Koreans removing cadavers was in stark contrast to the earth being churned up and releveled around them. The terrain itself looked like a wet and crumpled map.

In the photo I mentioned, I was skinny as a stick, but only four years later, after I completed my second enlistment as a paratrooper, I was iron hard and weighed one hundred sixty-five pounds. You could say I grew up in the army, and I couldn't understand why soldiers bitched about the food. I'd never eaten so good, and that included C rations and K rations, which all but gagged some GIs. The Korean *chogi*-bearers we hired as supplementary laborers shared my taste and, in fact, preferred to be paid in C rations.

I never could call Koreans who worked for us "gooks" like most GIs did. It reminded me too much of dad's bigotry. I tried to learn a little of their language and history. One day in Suwon, not far from Pyongtaek, I stared with awe at the remnants of an enormous wall that resembled the Great Wall of China. It stretched like a broken stone dragon over the hills.

I was astonished by what the *chogi*-bearers could do with the most primitive equipment. Using a simple A-frame platform, consisting of two stout limbs lashed together, they could load and carry phenomenal burdens. Their calves were knotted with muscles even as old men. I saw one stocky Korean carry a fifty-five-gallon drum of gasoline, more than two hundred pounds, that way.

I was assigned to the 1903rd EAB, or Engineer Aviation Battalion, whose combat engineers were specially trained to build airstrips. Marine Air Group 12 (MAG-12) was on the other side of the valley. It was for their Panther jets, prop-driven Skyraiders, and P-51 Mustangs that we were building the airstrip, designated K-6— the sixth U.S.-built air base in Korea.

Skyraiders were big, powerful planes painted dark blue with white markings, which, believe it or not, landed more lightly than jets. While the concrete runway inched forward through that freezing winter and on into March, all the planes used World War II pierced-plank steel runways.

Ted Williams, who had flown as a marine in World War II, flew a Skyraider in Korea (thus having his baseball career interrupted twice), and once, riddled by enemy flak, he made a crash landing on our strip. He came in low and slow, obviously crippled, and the moment his gear touched down, one of them crumpled and threw the plane over onto its back. We engineers watched the episode from a quarter mile away. Emergency crews quickly removed the famed athlete, who was hanging upside down. He wasn't hurt, but none of us ordinary mortals were allowed to visit him.

The marine contingent was there to guard the MAG and take care of any enemy guerrillas that might come along. It all sounded very romantic to a wide-eyed rube like me, but I was barely there a month before a marine sentinel was found with his throat sliced open, and that was the end of the romance. The base went on alert, and scouting patrols were sent out, but they found nothing.

My demolition squad had their twelve-man tents, and the marines had theirs, protected by earthen berms thrown up by bulldozers. We didn't mix except at the beer tent, at the rare times when there was beer. Mostly, we just worked. Twelve to sixteen hours a day was routine, more if weather allowed—or sometimes if it didn't allow.

As winter chewed into the frozen hills, we lit job-site fires in steel drums and periodically ran over to warm ourselves at them from whatever we were doing, like freezing hoboes. No wood was available except the crushed packing crates that machinery arrived in. But we did have plenty of Composition C-3, thanks to some supply sergeant's oversight. C-3 was a very stable explosive that, without primer cord or a blasting cap, would not detonate—although it would burn very hot for a long time. We powder monkeys were popular when we tossed chunks of this stuff, which the French call *plastique*, into a burning barrel. Not that we spent much time there. It was mostly dash to the flames, whip off the cumbersome gloves, warm our icy hands, and get back to the job. The days passed this way in frozen succession.

And then, one sunny arctic day, it was Christmas.

FOR A LONG TIME, I had another picture of me, this one taken with a Kodak Pony-135, standing by the Christmas tree. The battalion commander, an otherwise dislikable major, ordered the men to send Christmas pictures home. Like so many others, that photo has disappeared into the whirlpool of years.

Letters were the highlight of our lives and meant more than anyone back home could ever know. I got a few letters from mom, and perhaps two from my dad. I did get a Christmas package full of cookie crumbs. "Enough here for the whole company!" I shouted. "One crumb each!"

A couple of young women got my address from mom and wrote me gentle chit-chat that showed they were only vaguely aware of the war's reality but were doing their patriotic duty. Dad, making jets at Lockheed, apparently had neither time nor energy to write—or possibly even the inclination.

Most of my eleven months and sixteen days were served with resignation as I marked my calendar and wondered if I'd ever get back home. Engineers were there to work, and the infantry was there to fight, and that's pretty much the way things went—until we had enough rotation points to go home.

Late one November night, noncoms came running through the tents, shouting, "Out of those bags and to your posts! We're under attack!" I threw trousers and a field jacket over my long johns and slipped into my thermal boots. A dusting of snow had fallen earlier, and it was very cold. My heart was banging like a loose screen door. As the number-two man on a .30-caliber machine gun, I was tense and scared. We were in a zone free of enemy forces, but guerrilla bands sometimes got through and raised hell. Actual combat along the front line, or Main Line of Resistance (MLR), was in a lull. But soon it would be 1953, and some of the worst fighting of the war would rage all along the MLR as both sides tried to cement their gains. But before 1953, fighting was mostly confined to probing patrols as the Panmunjom peace talks dragged on.

My buddy and I sandbagged the gun behind the berm, with the barrel just above it. All along the earthworks, I saw dark shadows against white snow, men running to positions, machine gunners and riflemen getting ready—guys barely out of high school preparing for battle and possible death. There was a long period of silence. Then, somewhere a rifle cracked—and that was all it took. Machine guns and automatic rifles ripped the night open, and tracer bullets floated through the air like fireflies. The turbulent clatter continued for a couple of minutes despite the "cease fire!" shouts of sergeants and officers. When it finally stopped, the silence was thunderous. We stayed there, freezing, with only a dirgelike wind for company until, an hour later, we were allowed to hobble back to our tents.

In the chow line next morning, a PFC remarked, "They found two dead gooks out in the paddies." He didn't say whether they were soldiers or civilians, but no one seemed to know or care, so numbed were they by labor and stress. We were trying to speed the airstrip's completion date and were working even harder. My demolition team and I blasted all day long, making big rocks into little ones with dynamite, C-3, and TNT. Morale was low and stayed low until our battalion commander took an R and R to Japan to meet his wife, a WAC captain.

Twenty-four hours after the major and his wife departed, we got the surprise of our lives. Not only did a beer truck from Seoul arrive with excellent Asahi beer, but a bus loaded with prostitutes followed. I never learned who took it upon himself to throw the party, but it sure wasn't the major. It boosted morale in a big way, although a one-liter bottle of beer was all it took to anesthetize my pint-sized body. When a woman came by and cooed, "Make-e love, GI boy?" I was too sleepy to even answer. A good thing, too, since several cases of clap were spawned by that party.

New Year's Day, 1953, came and went. The Christmas tree was taken down, and work on the airstrip went on, twenty-four hours a day. Finally, late in still-frozen March, it was completed. For the next four months, until the truce was signed at Panmunjom, K-6 at Pyongtaek was a wasp's nest of roaring Mustangs and hissing jets, all headed north to fight MIGs and bomb North Korea. This was the bizarre nature of things as peace talks went on over an unbelievable two-year span.

SOMETIMES AT NIGHT, so tired I couldn't sleep, I would wrap a GI blanket around me and step out of the tent to look at the long, gray concrete runway and the work lights decorating the lonely valley in this strange, beautiful country I'd come to. A jewel-box sky was littered with stars, and a late-rising moon balanced on the horizon like a Chinese lantern. Strange country? We were the ones who were strange. How would it would feel to be in America and have three million foreign soldiers loose in our country? Were it not for the people's straw-roofed homes and their quaint costumes, this could have been the plains of Nebraska—for the only hills near us were low and rolling. At night, moonlight made them resemble a surging ocean.

One night, enough snow had fallen to turn the moonlit valley into a silver sea, a scene of such desolate beauty it froze my heart with loneliness. What were we doing here? What was any soldier doing in any war? Politicians made them, generals ran them, soldiers died in them. And even though I didn't know it in 1953, this pointless war would still be stalemated half a century hence, when I, now twenty, would be an old man.

In the frozen hills beyond the MLR, the enemy tried to keep warm, tried to find enough to eat, tried to kill Americans just as we tried to kill them. Who gets these things started? Enemy or not, they were like us. They did what they were told in the name of God, country, and the chain of command. But somehow, out of all the mindless conflicts, we never learned how to remain at peace for long.

Finally, the cold drove me back inside, where I lay thinking for a long time, a boy surrounded by snoring boys. I wondered about so many things. Life not only wasn't fair, most of the time it didn't even make sense.

WITH THE AIRSTRIP COMPLETED and in operation, my demolition squad was given another assignment—carving a road to the top of a mountain where a USAF radio relay site was going to be installed.

As we were assembling our gear, we got the news that a demolitions specialist from another unit had died while removing mines. An infantryman said that one of the man's arms, torn loose by the blast, fell off at the aid-tent door. Years later, that story led to "Shellshock":

> I am MacFatridge as he was then,
> Torn by the mine he was defusing;
> At the aid-tent door his arm fell off,
> And a medic stooped to retrieve it
> And stood as though lugging a melon
> That had burst in the sun.

There are those of us who are not tough
Despite all they told us. If I cry
Now, no one seems to care, but before,
I would have been punished with a laugh.
I wish that underneath the green sky
Of this room, images of terror
Would come again: that the emerald door
I can't pass would let me out to sleep.

The road we were to build to the relay site, which bounced radio transmissions the length of Korea, would be a permanent one—which delighted the air force technicians manning it. Far from military protection, they were sitting ducks on a giant rock pile. A road would allow them to expand and bring in some marines to help guard the place.

I've forgotten the exact location, but I think it was south and east of Seoul, maybe seventy-five miles from Pyongtaek. The mountain itself looked down on a wide plain of dead, yellow fields in winter and jade-green paddies in the spring. A ribbon of dusty road traversed it. I could have been looking at Kansas.

Korea is known as the "Land of the Morning Calm," and in late spring, its beauty fits the description. Its mountains have huge boulders embedded in them, and between these and smaller rocks grow a king's ransom in floral jewels.

It was slow-going through the hard rock as the big D-8 Cats spiraled slowly up the mountain, dozing the rubble produced by the charges we had exploded. We bored holes in the cliffs and tamped dynamite in with wooden poles. I holed each firing-stick of dynamite with a sharp crimping tool and then carefully eased a blasting cap two inches into it. That was my job, performed alone, with the others far back. When everything was ready, our lieutenant shouted, "Fire in the hole!" and our Korean liaison echoed, "*Nahm-po!*" Then I hunkered down below the road's edge and twisted the detonator's handle. A shattering *crru-u-mmm-ppp!* followed as we crouched low, holding our steel helmets down as rocks pelted the earth around us.

The mountain was steep, with scant vegetation and plenty of snow, even in April. We slept in pup tents on-site while the airmen lived and worked in a big Quonset hut. We combat engineers envied their laid-back lives, which, as near as we could tell, consisted mainly of manning radios in a heated hut. In one of those strange encounters that war and life are noted for, I ran into one of the men three years later at a military base in Texas. Like me, he couldn't find a job after Korea and had reenlisted in the air force, deciding to make it a career.

There's a Korean folk song called "Arirang" that I learned from a *chogi*-bearer. It's about a mountain that deliberately becomes steeper to thwart an unfaithful husband's attempt to visit his mistress on the other side. The husband tries to get Arirang Mountain to change its mind, but to no avail. That folk song's lament mirrored how we felt about the mountain where we were constructing our road, but without the enticement of a beautiful woman on the other side. Paris Mountain (the platoon commander swore that was its name) seemed to get steeper as we blasted, dug, laid culverts, and dynamited rock cliffs. Far below us, a flat plain, quilted by family farms and paddies, endured its ration of snow, rain, and eventually sun.

Sometimes I would think of the Alcan Highway, a remarkable engineering feat of World War II. Our road was a trail compared to that one, but our blisters were real. We lived on C-rations, which the Koreans loved and would trade labor for. They made cigarette lighters from the cans and sold them back to us. A Korean barber even gave us velvet-smooth shaves, using half of a thin Gillette razor blade held between his fingers.

IN MID-JUNE, I was banged around by a major dynamite charge. We had seeded a stubborn cliff above a forty-eight-inch culvert, but when I twisted the handle of the ten-cap detonator, nothing happened. I waited several minutes and then examined the charge. Nothing was wrong, so the trouble was in the detonator.

Our platoon lieutenant, Bob something-or-other, wasn't a demolitions specialist, but an eccentric Texan who wore his .45 automatic in a cross-draw position. We liked anyone who thumbed their nose at regulations, and even better, Lieutenant Bob didn't try to be an officer. He was easygoing and let us do the jobs we'd been trained for. (Now that I reflect, he might have been a little lazy, too.)

"Well, Corporal, what do we do now?" he asked.

I thought about the problem for a minute. Then I said, "If I can lug a jeep battery into that culvert, and you can pass the wires in to me, I think I can blow the cliff."

He looked at me curiously. "How would that work?"

"Batteries have positive/negative poles, and that's what's required to complete a circuit through the wires to fire the blasting caps. It's the same principle that creates lightning."

I wasn't completely sure it would work, but he agreed to give it a try. So I crammed my one-hundred-twenty-pound body into the five-foot galvanized steel culvert directly under the blast site, and the jeep battery was passed in to me. After a suitable wait to make certain everyone was clear, I got set and shouted, "Fire in the hole!" and a distant Korean voice echoed, *"Nahm-po!"*

I touched the bare wires to their respective battery poles, and with thunder I can still hear, the world caved in. Unfortunately, I had seriously underestimated the two hundred pounds of dynamite in the cliff's face. It went off like a thousand-pound bomb. I was much too close to the powerful blast, and even though protected by a steel culvert under three feet of earth, I went rattling around the big steel tube like a marble in a jar. Thick, choking dust poured in. The battery broke, and acid burned my legs and dissolved my fatigues. They were so tattered when I emerged, Lieutenant Bob thought my flesh had shredded.

"Jesus! You all right?" he yelled, rushing up as I crawled, stunned and coughing, into the sunlight. I couldn't get my bearings at first, but one of my squad, seeing the acid spill on my legs, immediately emptied his canteen over the area to dilute it. I would walk gingerly for a few days but suffered no lasting damage—except to my hearing. Dizzy, disoriented, bleeding from my nose and right ear, and knowing I was lucky that the concussion hadn't killed me, I stood up. The end of the culvert nearest the blast was buried under tons of rock. The next day, my body would be so sore from bouncing off corrugated steel I could barely move.

As soon as lieutenant Bob saw that I was going to live, he shouted enthusiastically, "Corporal, that took a lot of guts! I'm putting you in for the Bronze Star!" Some of the men heard him say it and later told me I deserved it. But Lieutenant Bob must have forgotten, because that was the last I ever heard of any Bronze Star. However, medals didn't always mean what they were supposed to in Korea.

According to Martin Russ's excellent Korean War book, *Breakout*, Major General Edward Almond, already considered a fool and a sybarite by the marines and by General Omar Bradley, "Put three Silver Stars in his field jacket pocket and told Colonel Don Carlos Faith he wanted to give them out before he left [the front] where he was visiting." Disgusted by this (the Silver Star, after all, is our third-highest military decoration), Faith chose himself, a mess sergeant, and a wounded lieutenant, the rest of the company being on patrol. As soon as Almond was back on his helicopter, Faith ripped the medal from his own jacket, as did the others. "What a goddamn travesty," he muttered. Faith would later be killed in action. Almond, at one time MacArthur's chief of staff, would retire to his home in Alabama.

Years later, when I had accumulated experience with corporations, I realized that I shouldn't have been surprised. The army is a giant corporation, with many ambitious people trying to claw their way to the top, or earn an extra star—and not always caring how they do it. Decades later, with my hearing seriously affected, the Veteran's Administration refused to give me hearing aids. I had to buy my own. Lieutenant Bob had apparently not even written a report about my unique blasting methods.

BY MID-JULY, exhausted by round-the-clock labor and wondering what the hell it was all for, we were bitter and demoralized. We'd been road building for three months. The talks at Panmunjom and the daily air attacks were still going on. Thoughts of soldiers dying while the flap-mouthed brass on both sides yammered on (mind you, nothing was gained by this war, on either side) infuriated us and affected morale. I fantasized a huge bomb falling on Panmunjom, turning all the generals into hamburger.

Rumors of a near truce reached us, but jets still rippled through the skies. In war, of course, only a relative few do the actual fighting. The rest are support troops. The road was almost completed, but we knew there'd be something else after that, some plan planned by the planners, with their meetings and pointers and self-important airs. The days spun on as summer's web of sunshine tendriled the mountain we were on.

One day, a Korean *chogi*-bearer who spoke broken English informed me that people were starving in the village at the mountain's base. "No more fish," he said, shrugging his shoulders. "River all fished out. Maybe some long way down, in pools we not reach."

Dad and Uncle Tom, not to mention other farmers, had often thrown half sticks of dynamite into pools where "big ones" were said to lurk. The concussion affected the fishes' air bladders, and they floated helplessly to the surface. I told Lieutenant Bob about the situation in the village, explaining that I wanted to fill some empty C-ration cans with Composition C-3. "We don't use it much on this job," I said, "and we have a ton of the stuff." He agreed, and with half a dozen cans stuffed with the yellow *plastique* and ten-second-delay waterproof fuses attached, the Korean and I jeeped down the mountain and through the little village to the river winding past it.

"Over there is deepest pool," my guide said. As I took the explosives and got out of the jeep, people started gathering, so I told him they should get back in case the blasts kicked up rocks from the riverbed. This was fine diplomacy, as it allowed him to assume a position of importance he'd never had before, and he availed himself of it with energy. I caught the word *nahm-po* (dynamite), but that was all of his lecture I understood as I studied the deep green pool and lined up my potent C-rations. Then I signalled my ally who, as pompously as any CEO, yelled, *"Nahm-po!"*

The white-clad people scattered like windblown confetti, and I remember well the scene that followed my dropping of the first can.

Perhaps you've seen those tall green cypress trees like giant exclamation points without the dot? That was the shape we saw when the first *whummpp!* came from below the water. Up, up, up rose the silvery plume as the villagers stared in awe. I had unwittingly created tiny shape-charges. The C-ration cans shaped the explosion into a seventy-foot column of shining water.

Then came the fish, raining out of the sky, and the cheering began. By the time all the little bombs had gone off, and all the silver columns had climbed, every basket in the village was full. The fish would be dried and divided and hopefully would last until the rice crop came in.

The plight of civilians is a problem that is seldom thought about much in war. Yes, soldiers suffer and die, but the civilian population—which includes babies and children—dies in far greater numbers, and often in greater agony, than do soldiers.

The mayor, a tall old man with a black stovepipe hat and wispy whiskers (Koreans are relatively beardless until elderly), came up to me, executed a dignified bow, and said, *"Koom-op-soom-ne-dah, Nahm-po-dingi-nodangi."*

I looked at my guide, who explained: "He say, 'Thank you beautifully, dynamite man with golden hair.' Great honor for you." And such I've always considered it. My months in the Land of the Morning Calm weren't all bad.

A TERRIBLE ACCIDENT happened two nights later when a Cat driver, exhausted from hours on the seat of his jolting D-8, stopped the huge tractor for refueling. But he forgot to let the diesel motor cool down before putting gasoline in the donkey engine that's used to crank the big bulldozers. There was a soft *whoof,* like a parachute opening, and he turned into a fountain of fire. He leaped screaming from the tractor and ran into the night. Flames blown by the wind of his passage looked like fluttering wings. Half a dozen men tackled him and rolled him in field jackets to smother the flames.

Terribly burned and out of his head with pain, he wept and moaned, even after our medic injected morphine. We got on the

SCR-300 and radioed, and thirty minutes later a marine helicopter was hovering overhead. There were no lights on the mountaintop, and the only landing space was surrounded by rotor-shattering boulders. The pilot literally had to thread the needle, guided only by a ring of men holding flashlights. In the dust kicked up by his rotor blades, the lights looked like wavering fireflies.

What a pilot! He brought the Sikorsky H-19 in amid a swirl of dust and pinging gravel, and we loaded our moaning casualty aboard. But he was too badly burned, and shock would kill him before he reached the medical unit. To this day, I can't recall his face—only the human torch lighting the midnight sky on a godforsaken hilltop in Korea.

Trying to Remember People I Never Really Knew

There was that guy
on that hill in Korea.
Exploding gasoline made him
a thousand candles bright.
We guided the Samaritan 'copter
in by flashlight
to a rookery of rocks,
a huge, fluttering nightbird
aiming at darting fireflies,
and one great firefly
rolling in charred black screams.

There was the R.O.K. soldier
lying in the paddy,
his lifted arms curved
as he stiffly embraced death,
a tiny dark tunnel over his heart.
Such a small door
for something as large as life
to escape through.

Later, between pages and chapters
of wars not yet written up
in Field Manuals or Orders of the Day,
there came shrieking down
from a blue Kentucky sky
a young paratrooper whom technology failed.
(I must correct two common errors:
they are never called shroud lines,
and paratroopers do not cry Geronimo.)

I wish I could say
that all three men fathered sons,
that some part of them still lived.
But maybe I don't, for the children's ages
would now be such as to make them
ready for training as hunters of men,
to stalk dark forests
where leaden rain falls with a precision
that can quench a hunter's fire.

IT'S ONE OF THE GIVENS of war that some plans fail and much materiel will be wasted, and so it was with our mountain road. Rough, rocky, but passable, with shining culverts in place, it was completed just days before July 27, 1953, when a truce put the Korean War on hold—where it's been ever since. The road, if it's still there, is probably paved now, with the condos of rich Koreans lying at its end atop that god-awful mountain.

One mail call brought a letter from my dad—the second and last one I got from him in Korea. (I only remember ever receiving one other, making three in a lifetime.)

Well, Bill, how are you? We are all well here. We are in California now. I work at Lockheed making jets. Your mother cleans houses. The other day she cleaned Gene Autry's. Well, Bill, there is no news.

Goodbye, Dad

ON A SUN-POLISHED AFTERNOON, I spotted a plume of golden dust trailing a speeding jeep in the valley far below. Soon it was grinding up the slope as fast as it could. Reaching us, the driver leaped out, a crazy grin on his face.

"The war's *over!*" he yelled. "The war is over, and we're goin' home!" Like a magician, he whipped back a tarp that covered cases of beer. Cheers rang from the rocks as sixty soldiers and airmen converged and started opening the big brown bottles of Asahi, Japan's top beer. Since it was warm (not that we cared), some went off like my fish bombs. We laughed and sang in a kind of delirium, partying deep into the night before staggering to our sleeping bags.

By August 16, 1953, I was officially a short-timer, marking on a calendar the agonizingly slow passage of days—days that, when I grew old, would bullet past like the long-ago snipes in that Oklahoma pasture. Then one day, the CQ ran to the latrine where he'd seen me headed and yelled, "Childress, your orders just came!" I left the latrine like a rocket, packed my gear, and boarded a Military Air Transport Service plane to Sasebo, Japan—and there, a final wartime experience etched itself into my mind.

I was lying on my bunk one day, waiting on a ship and reading. I heard a trickling sound and saw a soldier get up from a far bunk and slip out of the room. The trickling went on, but a look around showed me nothing. What was going on?

I had just risen to investigate when two MPs and a pair of medics burst in with a stretcher and rushed to a corner bunk. All hell broke loose as a sergeant first class leaped up from the bunk and began fighting them. He was a ghastly sight, drenched in blood, with more spurting from the grinning mouth he had razored into his left wrist. Naked from the waist down, he wore only a khaki shirt adorned with medals and a tie. A large man, he grappled with the MPs, and a grisly dance ensued with the trio fighting in silence. The MPs' uniforms were soon blood-soaked.

One of the medics shouted frantically, *"Hold him! I can't get the goddamn tourniquet on unless you hold him!"* The MPs finally wrestled the soldier to the floor. I saw that he wore a combat infantryman's badge above the Korean War medals on his shirt. Among them was a Silver Star, which is given for gallantry in action. He was subdued, finally, tourniqueted, strapped to a stretcher, and carried out—but he died later from shock and loss of blood.

Small wonder. The one-gallon butt can by his bunk, where he chain-smoked as his life drained away, was full of blood. The rest he had lost fighting for his death.

A bloodstained letter from his fiancée was found on his bunk. After surviving many combat patrols at the front, he had enough points to rotate home and marry the woman he'd gotten engaged to before shipping out. But her letter ended that dream. She wrote that she had fallen in love with another man and had already married him. She said she was sorry. She said it was probably the best thing for both of them.

Well, one of them anyway.

I NEVER HEARD of a general freezing to death in a Korean ravine, but I knew soldiers who did. The generals, warm and cozy in their rear echelon trailers, were the CEOs of the military. They had underlings to do everything from shining their boots to driving their cars.

These worthies come up with maneuvers like the one where, to show off for visiting congressmen, they ordered a regimental infantry attack on a Chinese-held hill. (It's in all the Korean War history books.) They ordered it twice, and it failed twice, and many kids my age died for nothing because these career-happy sons of bitches had power over them. I hope they impressed the members of Congress. Maybe that's why so many veterans shoved Korea out of their minds as quickly as possible.

Some didn't, or weren't able to. One veteran wrote, in material later published, "Our hatred of our government exceeds the furthest imaginable limits of human calculation." The writer died a hopeless drug addict a couple of decades later.

In 1999, W. D. Ehrhart, a poet and Purple Heart marine veteran of Vietnam, tried to bring the Korean War back to American memories by publishing an anthology of poems and stories, *Retrieving*

132

Bones. Both World War II and Vietnam had been much written about and honored. But the Korean War was ignored.

In Korea, the North Korean communists and their Chinese allies suffered 3 million casualties, and the forces of the United Nations 1.5 million. Most UN losses were soldiers from the Republic of South Korea. No territory was gained or lost, no peace treaty ever signed. Our soldiers today—including one of my sons, Buddy Roger Childress—still patrol the 38th parallel where the war started and ended, as they have for virtually my entire life. Korea's final legacy: It's called "the forgotten war."

"Forgotten?" wrote Columbia University's John Schulz in his January 2, 2000, *Chicago Tribune* review of *Retrieving Bones.* "Suppressed is the word. Rushed off the center stage of history and into the wings."

The fiftieth anniversary of the Korean War was in 2003. I hope everyone remembered that Truman's "police action" took thirty-four thousand American lives in less than three years. Vietnam needed ten years to equal that body count.

THE KOREAN WAR was already forgotten when the USS *Simon Bolivar Buckner* docked in Seattle in mid-September 1953. There wasn't even a Red Cross doughnut wagon to meet the wall of olive drab uniforms lining the rail. The war had been over for six weeks, plenty of time for Americans to forget, and our reward was that the be-shitten navy gave us thirty days of KP while we waited to be shipped to Fort Ord, California, our place of separation.

No one wanted anything to do with Korea, past, present, or future. It was this attitude more than any state of exhaustion that embittered me. Why the hell should any soldier fight to defend such citizens? I know from talking to veterans of the Vietnam War that many of them held similar views. Discharged and home, I was moody, angry, and depressed for weeks. Mostly, I slept in the tiny basement room the family let me use. Nobody ever asked about Korea. I drifted into a brief phase of playing "catch up," trying to recapture what I felt I'd missed in a year and a half. I drank, brawled, roared around in a 1938 Ford Coupe I bought for fifty dollars, and chased women. I never caught any, though, which only added to my dark moods. On one date, I mentioned to the girl that I was a veteran of Korea.

"Korea?" she said, a blank look on her face. "What's that?"

4

TRAVELING BY AIR, and I've done plenty, is a little like being a goldfish. You're suspended in a metal aquarium with Plexiglas holes, peering out at a world of clouds or cerulean sky. The clouds below you don't appear to be moving, except when the sun strikes them just right, and the plane's shadow skips over their surface like a flat rock skittered across water. Then gaps open to reveal the earth, all gold and crimson and black, and I think back to all the Ozark autumns when I stood outside watching lines of geese stenciling the Ozark sky. Fall is the time for musical migrations, symphonies of bird voices, especially those of geese. They fill the heavens like flights of dark arrows.

Nothing has ever stirred my heart like the cries of wild geese. Nothing ever will. There is something about the sound that speaks freedom, a freedom no mortal can ever know. Of the twice-yearly passage of these wonderful birds, spring is the time I like best. From their autumn flight, ambushed by hunters, many will not return. But in the springtime, itself a time of rebirth and renewal, theirs is the symphony that heralds a brave new world. Their music does not diminish though humanity is so careless with that world. Their songs do not grow less as wetlands dry up because of greed and exploding populations. The wild geese go on doing their jobs, trusting that we will do the same.

High overhead, so far up that arcs of birds drift like gossamer threads against a garter-blue sky, the band tunes up. Then another wave chimes in, lower down. And another. Their songs merge as a hoarse, melodious, "Move along, move along!" And moods improve all over the place. Each voice is alike yet different, and no doubt a trained musical ear could pinpoint an off-key oboe, a small tuba, or a somewhat hoarse trumpet. To me, the sounds are simpler, yet too noble to be called *honking*. I have never been satisfied with that label. Cars honk—geese cry out with guttural joy, singing a song of flight and freedom conducted by some inner baton. It's a call that echoes in the high, blue canyons of the sky, a call still tied by some thread of instinct to the geese of long ago and to ancestors still more remote. When the clocks inside them were being set by the seasons, our feeble civilization did not exist. How perilous that the human race, a latecomer to nature's script, should now be their worst enemy—as it has always been its own.

Every autumn and spring for over six decades, the wild geese have measured my life. For the first few years, I never heard them, or else paid them little mind. For the next few, busy with growing up, I saw them only as beacons of passing years, pushing towards that magic time when I would be twenty-one and free, a wild goose of my own. How fast I've flown on the wings of my life since then!

I had it all figured out. First, escape the shackles of the farm, the dawn-to-dusk labors, the balky mules, the endless attempts to satisfy parents whose only vision was locked into bills and crops and groceries. Only when I became a parent myself did I understand my own much better. But sometimes I wonder, now that both of them are gone, if they ever heard a mystery in the cry of a wild goose, or in its haunting plea to move along, move along, move along. Perhaps like me, my folks had questions all their lives about the meaning of life, before finally accepting it for what it is: a miracle that defies definition.

Like wild birds, we take our portion and shape it the best way we can, and if sometimes it's as shapeless as those ragged lines of geese, we must try to find beauty in it still. I think that was why, in midlife, I returned to the Ozarks. Just as something in Canada calls the geese home in the spring, something in these hard old hills keeps tugging at my heart. It's as good an explanation as any.

NOW THE MOMENT I'd dreaded had come. My last living parent was dead, and I was coming home to the little town of Anderson, Missouri, where dad would be buried next to mom, and where I had spent nearly one-third of my life.

The flight from St. Louis to Springfield took an hour, and it was two o'clock by the time I rented a car, a maroon Toyota, and headed out on Highway 60 west. I figured I could reach Anderson by dusk—due to come early this cool October day. From there, it would take me another half an hour or so to reach dad's trailer, which sat by Grand Lake o' the Cherokees near Grove, Oklahoma, twenty-four miles from Anderson. The car purred smoothly through the autumn countryside. To my left, a phalanx of trees bursts from the ground like golden fountains, and a herd of Holsteins make Rorschach patterns in the pasture.

Dad, dead since yesterday, waited in the Ozark Funeral Home in Anderson for final interment in Split Log Cemetery, just down the road from the farm he owned for over thirty years. He'll lie beside mom, who died in 1992 at the age of seventy-nine. Dad bought the plots and headstones years ago, making sure that he and mom would be together in death as they were in life—only more quietly. I could almost see the old man smile. "Your mother gets things backwards," he once confided. "She thinks the storm should come before the calm." Theirs was a union of agitation and strife, with mom's temper on top and dad's buried deeper but available before you knew it. Now they had the peace they'd always craved.

I found this stretch of Highway 60 much improved in the years since I'd last driven it, with thick black asphalt and easy-to-see road stripes. At one time, many deaths were caused by its uneven hills and curves. Highway 60 is not a minor byway. It crosses the nation from Newport News, Virginia, to Los Angeles, California, and few highways have such a cornucopia of sights, ranging from the Allegheny and Appalachian Mountains to the Ozarks. I traveled both directions on it many times. Of the two thousand or so stories I wrote over thirty-seven years, many came from Highway 60.

Long before I became a travel writer, I drove Highway 60 from Richmond to Los Angeles. After the Korean War ended, before I reenlisted in the paratroops, I used my GI bill to go to barber college in Los Angeles—dad's idea, and a bad one. Needless to say, though, he wasn't so dumb conning me into barber school—I ended up cutting his hair—free—for twenty years.

Barber training was basically boring, but there were occasional diversions by the master barber who taught the thirty-two ex-GIs and eight others in the school. Like the time he got into it with a skid row bum (we practiced haircuts and shaves on winos), and the two of them went to Fist City. The master barber accepted a left to the eye, then presented the bum's jaw with a right hook, and while the guy was stumbling around woozily, grabbed him by his belt and collar and evicted him. We had a new respect for the master barber after that.

Meanwhile, dad and mom had settled in the San Fernando Valley—which, in 1954, was filled with lettuce fields from horizon to horizon. Today, it's an ocean of rooftops. I didn't live at home; I stayed in a skid row hotel, which was reasonably clean and cost $7 a week.

One day, I was coming back from the bathroom in the rear of the forty-chair school and saw a new student frantically dumping styptic powder on a sleeping bum's ear—or what was left of it. Half the ear was lying on the floor amid unswept hair and bits of neckpaper. To give the kid credit, he knew how to sharpen a straight razor. When he slipped and took off the bum's ear, the guy snored on.

But when the styptic powder started stinging, he opened his eyes, saw the blood and the frantic student barber, and levitated from that chair like a helium balloon. The next thing I knew, he was running down the street with the bloody barber's cloth flapping behind him and the master barber in hot pursuit, yelling to the poor guy that he'd get him a doctor. But given the chintziness of the long-defunct American Barber College, we figured he just wanted the cloth back.

AFTER A SECOND STINT in the armed services, I got out for good in 1959. Discharged in Richmond, I ran into a short, graying man and mentioned that I was looking for work. He asked what I could do.

"Well, I'm just out of the paratroops," I said. "I cut a lot of hair in the army, and I went to barber college in California, but I don't have a license."

"Well, if that don't beat all!" the man said. "I just happen to own a two-chair barbershop, and my second barber quit a month ago. I'll try you out and see how you do. Got a specialty?"

"Flattops," I said.

"You take the back chair," he said.

Two months later, tired of averaging $25 a week when my boarding house was costing $35, I told the owner I'd had enough. My mustering-out money was almost gone, and I was looking right into the mouth of hard times. Besides, he didn't need two barbers; there wasn't enough business for one—and hardly anyone in Richmond wanted flattops. I was also homesick for my family.

As I packed up at the boarding house, a teacher who also stayed there came to my room and said, "I understand you're leaving. I'm sorry to hear it."

"I'm hoping the job situation will be better on the West Coast," I said. She was about ten years older than me, and since I had begun to do some "writing," I asked if she'd read it. She said yes, she would be happy to; and sometime later, she slipped it back under my door while I was retrieving my tools at the shop.

"A very impelling story," she had written. It was about packing patients in ice as anesthesia for surgery, and anyone who's had a wart removed with liquid nitrogen knows I was years ahead of my time. But the teacher's calling it "a very impelling story" didn't help. I needed someone to be critical. Eventually, I discovered that most teachers, unless they're published writers, are strangers to creative writing.

A COUPLE OF DAYS before I quit barbering, I was walking on a side street and saw an old gentleman standing in his garage, moodily contemplating a car. The garage lights were on, and I saw, up on blocks, a beautiful 1946 Packard, gleaming black and looking as new as the day it was bought. (I would later find out that it only had five thousand miles on it.) I loved old cars (having lived with lots of them growing up), and we began talking. He was a frail-looking man with white hair, pale eyes, and thick glasses.

"That's a beautiful car, sir," I said.

He peered at me, trying to focus on a blond-haired Dane with blue eyes, a flattop, and an Ipana smile. "You think so, do you?"

"Yes, sir. A Packard, ain't it?"

"A 1946 straight-six with the works," the old gent said. "But I developed cataracts ten years ago, and it's been up on blocks ever since. You like it?"

"Yes, sir!"

"You want to buy it?"

My eyes almost popped out of their sockets. "Don't I wish!" I exclaimed. "But all I have left is my mustering-out pay, and that ain't much."

"How much you got?"

Gloomily, I said, "A hundred and twenty-five bucks." I knew the car was worth double that and probably more.

He studied me long and carefully through his coke-bottle lenses. He looked to be about eighty. "You say you just got out of the service?"

"Yes, sir, about two months ago."

"Well, I'll never be able to drive it again," he said, with resignation in his voice. "And I think it'll give you many a good mile—so give me the $125, son, and it's yours." The old man was almost crying when I left, which made me almost cry, too. I had paid him all I had and thanked him from the bottom of my heart.

That Packard was a beauty, but like a fool—I'd never owned a car—I neglected to check the oil, forgetting that the old man told me it had not been driven for ten years. But with a newly charged battery, it started right up and drove like a limousine. Fortunately, it didn't have much gas in it, so with my last $25 from the barbering job, I pulled in to a gas station. The attendant studied the oil dipstick and said, "What have you got in here, molasses?" He drained it and put in a new filter and oil, and I headed west from Richmond on Highway 60 with a light heart and a lighter wallet. It was 1959. It would take me two months to reach Los Angeles, earning gas money as I went.

MY FIRST JOB was screeding concrete on a highway being built near Cache, Oklahoma, where Uncle Hamp was still farming the bottom land farm he leased. He was just a couple of years from moving to Missouri, where he would raise championship hogs. I worked on the highway crew for three weeks at $1.25 an hour. That was good in 1959, when gas was 20¢ a gallon, and it certainly beat the Richmond barbershop. But the foreman saw fit to question my screeding ability, making me think he had a nephew in the wings. So I told him that any career beat this one and let the handle of my screed drop on his toes. Time has proved me wrong, though. Construction pays lots better than writing.

OVER THE NEXT TEN YEARS, I got married, started a family, traveled around a good deal, and continued to write. Then in 1969–70, I spent a year at *National Geographic* as an editor-writer but soon grew tired of the gray-flannel minds of the ultraconservatives running the magazine (described by one writer as "tuxedo in front, nothing behind"). I honestly felt the bad vibes there, camouflaged behind hypocrisy and politics—the latter available just a few blocks away at the White House. There, "Tricky Dick" Nixon sat behind a ring of buses, watching football, while 250,000 protesters from all over America—including me, a Korean War veteran—marched for two days and nights against the Vietnam War.

When I left Washington in 1970, I thought, "Surely, California will be less stifling." But this was the time of the John Birch Society. The first day I reported to Allen Hancock College in Santa Maria, where I'd been hired to teach journalism, I found a brown-paper-wrapped book in my mailbox. It was J. Edgar Hoover's communist-scare book, *Masters of Deceit*. I burst out laughing, and a teacher next to me, seeing the book, said, "Better read it. Old man Hancock gives every new teacher one." At that time, the founder of Hancock Oil and, I think, the college was in his nineties, and in the opinion of most teachers, a delusional old man who saw communists under every bed.

"You ought to see him when he comes into town," another teacher said. "He has two Oriental karate-trained bodyguards riding the fenders of his Rolls Royce!"

The more I became part of the Establishment, the more I understood why young people were so much against it. Meanwhile, dad and mom were living in a little town a hundred miles northeast of Fresno State College, where dad ran a plumbing business. My sisters and brother were grown now and gone, as were the dusty, hard days on worthless farms.

"You like it out here?" I asked dad during one visit.

"Nope," he said. Sure enough, in a matter of months, he and mom left California to settle on their last Ozark farm—this time in Missouri. Dad was pushing fifty, and mom was fifty-two, but their fiddle-feet were still in operating order.

GROWING UP the son of a migrant worker and sharecropper means that your homes and your friends are few and far between. Often I would barely make a "best friend" when dad would uproot us, and we'd become road-toads again.

For some reason, the appeal of Anderson, Missouri, was different. It was there that he and mom settled in the mid-1960s, on a farm on F Highway, seven miles outside of town. And Missouri was where I came to create a simpler life when my California life was in shambles. Be it ever so humble, and it certainly was, Anderson was the place I came back to with a lifting heart each time a writing assignment was completed. It was a homely little burg with layers of feed-mill dust, cracked sidewalks, and nineteenth-century buildings. But it also had its beauty spots, like Town Hole down by the post office where, at age twelve, my son Chris once saved a boy from drowning.

Not to say that I lived on the hem of paradise—there were knocks aplenty. But that dusty little town became my first real home, with my first real friends. Folks gathered for picnics in the little park by the river. Here the grass was always green, and in the fall of the year, trees made the place look like a Jackson Pollock painting, all dribs and drabs of color. And the river water, until the poultry companies began polluting it, was crystal clear.

Like any small Southern town, Anderson had its share of ignoramuses. My first trip there had been in 1969, when I was still working at *National Geographic* and wore a beard. As I drove slowly through town, a pickup passed by, and a big, snaggletoothed woman with frizzy hair and little beady eyes banged on her truck's door and screamed, "Git outta town, hippie! We don't need yer kind here!" I guess she didn't notice the business suit and tie I was wearing. Later, I discovered she was the wife of a local rich rancher. A Republican, of course.

I SPENT twenty-four years of my life near my parents, joining the army at eighteen and returning to the Ozarks on my forty-first birthday. Eleven years of marriage and three sons later, wounded by life, I went back to the country ways that had bred me.

"Your dad is looking forward to your coming back here," said a letter from mom in 1972. "He says he'll sell you a few acres and help you get a trailer in. I know he will be happy to have more help on the farm."

When I arrived in the Ozarks with my three young sons, my dad was fifty-eight, and mom was sixty. Apparently, though, I hadn't aged along with them. When it came to work, dad gracefully deferred to my youth and let me dig a hundred or so postholes by hand.

It was 1973, and I was depressed by my California divorce from a beautiful woman I still loved, when I bought three wooded acres from dad and winched a sixty-five-foot trailer in among them. Black walnut trees, draped with vines as thick as my wrist, looked out across rolling pastures towards my parents' old farmhouse. Tucked behind a knoll a mile away, its pyramidal tin roof flashed like a semaphore in the afternoon sun. As the years passed, I would cross those pastures thousands of times to check on or assist my aging parents.

In those rolling meadows, summer daisies as white as buttermilk flowed towards dad's place, and my sons Chris, Jason, and David, later joined by my son from a second marriage, Buddy Roger, flew kites, skipped rocks across the cattle pond, and in general did the things kids do in a rural setting. My daughter Amanda, also from that second marriage (who recently gave me my first granddaughter, the lovely and talented Gwendolyn Rose), swung on vines like some tiny Tarzan.

The grove was a natural cathedral, draped with tapestries of leaves until fall, when black walnuts the size of tennis balls started dropping. During walnut gathering time, I wore a construction hard hat, having been struck and almost knocked out by the quarter-pound nuts. A lone cedar also occupies the grove, its top blown away by lightning and laced with possum grape vines. In the front yard sat a "cannon" one of my kids had fashioned from a hollow log and two old cultivator wheels.

For the next fourteen years, I lived there with and without my sons. The colors of the trailer changed with my moods and sometimes with the seasons. I became a literary hermit, the hippie in the Walnut Grove, a photojournalist often on some trip or other—France, Egypt, Israel, Machu Picchu, or Sri Lanka. The walnut trees were modest-sized when I moved in. They were giants when I returned to California twenty-four years later to marry a pen pal named Diane.

My kids loved the creeks, wildlife, fishing, and dad's old John Deere, but he was as gruff and aloof with his grandchildren as he'd been with his own children. They still adored him, sensing that the love his childhood made him incapable of showing lay just beneath the surface. Dad never believed that kids were the equal of adults. He believed that kids were *children*, and that children needed someone to guide them who was more father than pal. But times and parenting theories change. In any case, my kids have memories that will stay with them all their lives and hopefully anchor them when the seas of life get stormy.

Sometimes I took them with me on travel assignments. David went with me on the Lewis and Clark Trail. Jason biked with me across Iowa. Chris watched me photographing falcons in Oklahoma. I hope that visiting my world made up in part for my not always being in theirs. Both David and Buddy Roger later served in the military, David on a nuclear submarine, and Buddy as a heavy truck driver in Korea—just ten miles from where I blew things up as a demolitions specialist in the Korean War.

My kids are grown, now, as are the childhood friends who made the walnut grove ring with their laughter. The skinny little stick figures, happy voices, peanut butter raids, and broken windows are just memories. That's as it should be, because they're embarked on odysseys of their own, journeys I can't help them with, travels that must be theirs and theirs alone. May fortune bless them, because traveling can get rough at times.

WHEN IT COMES to survival, most liberal arts majors shun writing to pursue teaching. I did just the opposite. I meant to prove I could make a living at writing or starve. The Ozark Plateau—fifty-five thousand square miles of wooded wilderness laced by rivers—holds parts of seven states. It proved the perfect place for my inky adventures.

Compared to the East and West Coasts, the Midwest and South hadn't been much written about in 1973. Almost immediately I was making a living at my chosen trade, and in those simple days when all you needed was a typewriter and a ream of paper (not a hundred pounds of computer junk with $40 cartridges), I'd load my sons and a picnic basket into the pickup and head for Indian Creek. While they fished, swam, and tried to kill each other, I would drop my pickup's tailgate, set up my Hermes 3000 Portable, and get to work. I wish I had that Hermes now. It was Swiss made, by Paillard, I believe. Today, I sit in front of a glass screen with buzzings and hummings and things happening that I don't understand and can't fix. This damn computer eats words, too. One day it ate three thousand words, and I live in terror that some morning I'll turn it on and find that my book has disappeared. I never had that trouble with a typewriter.

When it comes to making a living, freelance writing is a hard row to hoe. So few survive at it that the U.S. government doesn't even recognize it as a profession. Ironically, in the Depression, some of our top authors got government jobs writing social history—still good reading today. But authors get other kinds of support, too. While living in the Ozarks, I received a letter in my mailbox that said, "We look at your books every day. They hold up a corner of our TV."

IT'S HARD TO BELIEVE I'll never be able to ask my parents a family-history question again. Mom never did talk much about her white-trash family, but I dug as deeply into both their lives as I could. Dad's life was also my life and the lives of his other children.

Although my parents and I lived separate lives when I returned to the Ozarks from California, they were always focal points for me as a writer. Dad in particular was the source of much family history, and since families are composed of individuals, and you never know what individuals are going to do, I saw a trove of regional literature ahead. I wrote both journalism and "literary stuff" (a novel, many short stories and poems), and I had to keep in mind what Oscar Wilde said about writing: "The difference between journalism and literature is that journalism is not readable and literature is not read."

Dad's memory seemed to improve with age. I'd question him about times long past and soon be writing about what it felt like to be freezing in a boxcar at fourteen, while fighting off a hobo who offered to keep you warm. Or watching tramps cook slumgullion in a rusty gallon can or make "chock," a deadly booze created by melting Sterno—anything to help them forget the misery of their lives. "It killed some of 'em," dad said. "It was wood alcohol. You couldn't pay me to drink that stuff."

He told of crashing headlong through hobo jungles with railroad bulls in hot pursuit, their truncheons raised high. When they caught up with a tramp, they would smash him in the head, and he would wake up in a filthy, sour-smelling jail, courtesy of the railroads. Then, according to dad, who went through it once, the tramp was driven to the edge of the city and turned loose with the words, "Don't let the sun set on your ass in this town again!"

"A lot of us, like me, was teenagers," dad said. "The railroads didn't give a shit, the thieving bastards. We wasn't worth nothin' to them, and more than one young kid was beat to death and left in a ditch. I've hated the railroad industry ever since. They stole a lot of taxpayer money and got away with murder, the bastards."

Dad was a registered Democrat, but there his interest in politics pretty much ended. He simply voted the straight ticket, never crossing party lines. In truth, though, he was very conservative, considerably so in later life. During his final years, I took recordings and notes by the hour, not knowing at the time that I'd later piece together his life from them but because his stories were fascinating. Recently, I played some of the old tapes, and his rumbling baritone floated across the years to me. He spoke haltingly about his side of the family, good folks mostly.

It was different, unfortunately, where mom's family was concerned. Grim experience had shown me that most of her kin were *not* good folks. They were thieves, heavy drinkers, gamblers, wife beaters, and, in general, the lowest kind of white trash. Yet mom loved them and was loyal to them—up to a point. Her mother and one sister were almost the only good ones in the whole family except for mom—a family I started avoiding decades ago. Several of the men went to prison. One died under the wheels of a train, where, it was believed, gamblers had thrown him. None of them, except mom, went past the second grade. Their father needed them to work in the fields.

Mom went to school for three years, growing up in the cotton fields with her brothers. There were seventeen kids in all, including a set of twins, and those who weren't in prison were bums most of their lives. Four died as infants. I put these facts down because

I don't want my kids to read the kind of sugarcoated history some folks prefer when it comes to talking about their forebears. People hide a lot that's better known than unknown. I didn't know until late in life that my maternal grandfather raped his eldest daughter in 1919. She had the baby, and grandma raised it. Poor Ruby never knew her mother. She grew up to be an alcoholic, married eight times. She was found dead in a Bakersfield motel, bludgeoned to death by her alcoholic eighth husband.

ONCE I CAUGHT DAD in the right mood and asked him to tell me about his side of the family, and he ended up giving perhaps the longest single speech of his life. Long for him, certainly, because he was a taciturn man.

"My grandpa was John William Childress of Tennessee," he began. "He was a judge who settled in Texas in the 1870s, intermarried with the Tiptons of Oklahoma, and had five sons—Will, Jim, John, Ray, and George E. Rastus Childress, my father. He also had four daughters, whose names I can't remember. I remember the boys' names because my own brothers had pretty much the same names.

"John William was a magistrate in Glen Rose, Texas, and died in his eighties in 1935—outliving my dad, who was forty-five when he died from a heart attack at the breakfast table in 1922. I was seven years old at the time. Jack, my youngest brother, had just been born. Six months later, our mother died from complications following the birth—I always knew it was a doctor's dirty hands that killed her. He liked his whiskey too much. They had bad doctors back then just like they do now.

"John William's sons were mostly professional people. Will was a Methodist preacher at a big church in New Orleans. He was a good, well-respected man with the ugliest wife I ever saw, although his kids were all good-looking. I never did figure that one out. Jim worked for a big grocery company in Abilene, Texas, and had a nice house. Ray was a school superintendent in Chillicothe, Missouri, and John worked as a railroad supervisor in Graham, Texas. Ray had a high opinion of himself and was real stuck-up. I never met his wife—

assuming he ever found a woman who could put up with him. Most people didn't like Ray because he acted too self-important.

"My daddy, George E. Rastus, was the only one to break away and become a farmer. He, Grandpa Childress, and Grandpa Tipton all had long beards, like the Smith Brothers on those cough drop boxes."

BY THE TIME DAD was born in 1915, almost a Christmas child, his father had become a successful and somewhat monied farmer in Oklahoma. "He knew how to farm," dad said. "He had one of the biggest, most successful farms in our county when he lived." But when he died suddenly in his mid-forties, it was found that the bank owned most of his success, and his pregnant wife inherited many debts. Every farmer knows it's a feast or famine business; the tragedy was that George E. Rastus Childress died during lean times. All the older sons gathered around to decide what to do. Three of them had already leased farms of their own, and Guy, the oldest, was in California, where he would work as a farmhand for the rest of his life.

Dad said a lot more that day, and in the end I knew more about his family than I'd learned in all the years I had lived with him. It was fascinating to realize that all these people were dad's kin but no blood relation to me. How much was accurate, I can't say, because dad was already approaching eighty. Still, he always had a clear, sharp mind.

It's enough to say that all of dad's brothers farmed on or near the Ozark Plateau as long as they could last without starving. Eventually, all but one were forced to move to the cities to find work. Over the years, America lost millions of farmers this way. My uncles ended up in Arizona, California, and Oregon. Only Uncle Hamp stayed in the Ozarks, raising hogs in central Missouri until his death in the 1980s. As the genial and henpecked older brother married to a religious wife, Hamp had taken dad and his sister Jo to raise—in dad's case, from ages seven to fourteen. But that was decades before Hamp moved to Missouri.

When he finally got his Missouri swine operation underway, it was the 1960s, and one day he came into the house with a pig so small that calling it the "runt of the litter" was an understatement. It wasn't much bigger than a teacup. Of course, his wife put her foot down—but for once Hamp stood his ground. The compromise was that Grunter (so named because he grunted constantly) could stay on the screened porch until he got big enough to compete with the other hogs. So Hamp made him a high-sided box and put some old quilts in it, and he nursed the tiny pig with a bottle till it finally took hold and began growing.

Hamp's truck was a rusty, banged-up old Ford that looked like it had been built by a shade-tree mechanic. No two fenders matched, the steering wheel had hunks of black rubber missing, the tires were balder than Grunter's belly, and the engine produced sounds of fierce combat when first started. He loved that truck. Regardless of the condition of his vehicles, Uncle Hamp ran a modern operation. On the Pokero place, many years earlier, our hogs had been fed kitchen slop—and some of the more enterprising farmers sought garbage from cafés, supplementing it with grain.

When I saw Hamp's place fifteen years after visiting him in Cache on my way to California, times had really changed. For awhile I thought I was in an agricultural testing lab. Fat, sassy pigs grunted and whuffed, nosing metal lids for grain or water, and nowhere was there any pig poop—a staple in the pens of my boyhood. This was progress with a capital *P*. The climate-controlled farrowing houses were marvels of imagination, pure hog-Hiltons.

I grew up when pigs were called *pigs*. The italics are mine, because on today's hog farms, you mustn't be too free with such nouns. *Pig* generally becomes *hog* among smaller farmers, while big companies raising thousands of animals prefer *swine*.

Uncle Bid, one of dad's older brothers, and Aunt Sam raised an orphaned Chester White in the 1940s and made it into a watch-pig. It was housebroken and took a proprietary interest in the place. On one occasion, after it was full grown, it came barreling out of the bedroom and chased a life insurance salesman clean off the premises. Aunt Sam was always proud of that. "It ain't life insurance, anyway," she said. "It's death insurance, and I sure don't need none o' that."

Hog raising was primitive when I was a kid. Our pigs had running water when it rained and air conditioning when the wind blew. But when it comes to quality of life, there ain't a pig in any of those fancy houses that wouldn't rather be out rooting for acorns in the oak woods.

SOMETIMES IN the Ozark Mountains, as twilight chases the sun to bed, the air is so clear and still it's like being under a Southern sea— an azure archipelago we can swim through in utter peace. The sky is like an enormous shell, pearly and lustrous, with strands of coral-tinted clouds strung across it. At such times, I think I could live in these billion-year-old hills ten times ten thousand years and never tire of them.

Nights, too, have a special magic in the Ozarks, and it doesn't matter what season it is. One midnight some years ago, I stepped out on my trailer's porch, feeling the crispness of fall in the air, drinking in the sights and sounds as I had so many times before. The loveliest sight among them was a strip of indigo blue skyline, shining with ghostly luster. The evening star was pinned just above it, the day's last hurrah. I remember wondering if I could ever leave the Ozarks. And then, one day, I decided I had to.

At the time, I was making a living writing, but just barely. I needed to find steady work. So, seven years after arriving in the hills, I took a job writing speeches for Phillips Petroleum executives in Bartlesville, Oklahoma. I lasted a year before the corporate miasma ripped out my soul, and I broke out of big oil's prison to run gratefully back to my woods. I came to the conclusion it was better to starve than to work with a bunch of corporate hypocrites whose sole raison d'être was to crush whatever creative spirit an individual has. My boss told me I was one of the best writers he had. But corporations don't want the best; they want the most pliant. The loss is everyone's.

I remember my only Christmas at Phillips Petroleum. It was 1980, and there was to be a Christmas party, and to me that spelled festivity, with folks letting their hair down a little. So I shelled out some hefty bucks for a Santa suit, strapped on a pair of pillows, and looked like I'd just touched down from the South Pole. Surely, no one would wear their gray-flannel armor tonight!

Surely they would. In fact, I was the only employee who *wasn't* in a suit and Korfam wingtips. Well, too late! Yodeling happy ho-ho-ho's, I walked in with my new wife on my arm, far and away the prettiest woman in the room. The entire room froze. All eyes were fixed on little old Santa Claus me. Then from the sidelines came a frightened, querulous voice:

"Does he have *clearance?*"

ONE DAY IN 1982, returning exhausted from a magazine assignment in El Paso, I arrived at the trailer just in time to hear my phone ring, and it was mom calling to say, "Well, he's broke down in El Reno and wants you to come and get him."

"Go *get* him?" I said. "I just got here! I'm dead beat!"

"Well, that's what he said to do. He's parked at a gas station on the highway, and he don't want to stay there all night."

"Why can't he catch a bus? That's what I had to do the last time I broke down in Texas. He sure as hell didn't come and get me!"

"I don't know a thing about it," mom said. "I told him that damn Chrysler was no good, but he bought it anyway. He never listens to me." That would be car number sixty-seven, since that was his age at the time.

I had two choices. I could listen to one of mom's harangues on the old man's contrariness, or go and get him. "I'll go get him," I said and hung up the phone.

Wearily, I climbed back into my car. El Reno is west of Oklahoma City, two hundred and fifty long miles from Anderson. It wasn't the first time I'd rescued my old man, nor would it be the last. To him, though, it wasn't even a question. I was the oldest kid, and the oldest kid always jumped through the hoop first.

DURING THE FOUR-HOUR TRIP to El Reno, I thought about dad's self-ish side. He definitely had one, and it was in good operating order right up to the day he died. Once, and only once, I asked him to lend me a thousand dollars that I very much needed. His response was gratifyingly prompt. "I ain't got it," he said, even though he had just sold a bunch of cows for good money. He would never lend me anything, not even his pickup if I needed to haul something. But damned if he wouldn't lend both truck and money to people who were a lot less kin to him than I was—and I wasn't any kin at all.

An example: One of mom's most worthless brothers was a bum named Homer. He had thinning hair, a flat, stupid-looking face, and tobacco-stained teeth. He was almost completely illiterate and possessed the genial air of an accomplished mooch. Dad had dealt with him before, may I add, and been stung worse than if he'd run into a yellow jacket's nest. Like most of his white-trash family, Homer was in and out of our lives and in and out of jail. He was also a child-abandoner and had a son (Homer Jr.) who, considering he'd spent most of his life *without* Homer, grew up to be amazingly like him.

One day Homer materialized out of nowhere, and after glad cries from mom, settled in to stay awhile. Dad was always easygoing about such things, even though none of mom's male kin ever did a lick of work—and in fact it was usually mom herself who got mad and told them to go find another free lunch someplace else. We once room-and-boarded mom's sister Ethel Timms and her worth-less husband and four kids, for an entire Oklahoma winter, strain-ing our meager budget to the limit. Even worse, while dad and I fought blizzards to feed our livestock, that sorry puke sat by the wood stove and spit tobacco juice on it until mom told him to use a spit-can or get the hell out.

On this visit, though, Homer vowed he was a better man. "I ain't had a drink in two months," he declared, and indeed his usual sal-low face and bloodshot eyes were nowhere in evidence. He even looked trim and sturdy.

"Why Homer, I'm proud of you!" mom replied, shooting dad a triumphant look, as if to say, "See? He doesn't drink *all* the time."

However, Homer wasn't just an alcoholic. Homer was a raging forest fire of an alcoholic. Over the years, we had seen (and heard) this many times. His benders were legendary and more than once had almost killed him. So his current condition was good news. Even I was impressed, when I came by for a visit, although I never had liked Homer and never would.

Mom put him in the spare room, and he set to work with dad. Over the next four weeks, he was a model of deportment. He got up, ate, went to work with dad, came home, ate, and after a little television, went to bed. Every so often we'd hear the sound of prayers from his room, which made dad look askance. He had long held that if Homer ever entered a church, the building would catch fire.

Dad and Homer built and repaired fences, hammered planks back on the barn, roofed the chicken house, cut and stored hay, and brush-hogged acre after acre. Then they went to the woods to cut and split winter firewood with dad's tractor-driven splitter. Against all odds, Homer was proving to be a godsend for both dad and me, since this was a busy time for me, and I was away too much for farm work. All this time, he had never gone into town or taken a drink. Eventually, dad was lulled into making another dumb decision: he trusted Homer with his new pickup—the same pickup that was off-limits to me!

"Homer, take the truck into town," dad said one day. "Get some chicken feed and livestock salt. It'll do you good to get off the place for awhile. Here's fifty bucks. That ought to cover everything."

"Well, okay, Jay, if you say so," Homer said and took the money and headed for Anderson. Once there, he went straight to the liquor store and bought a quart of Kessler Whiskey, his lifelong favorite. He didn't buy anything to dilute it with, either, as the owner told me later.

Back on the farm, dad was telling mom that sure enough, it looked like her rotten brother (*one* of her rotten brothers) had turned over a new leaf. "He's been a lot of help," he told mom, and mom beamed. She was loyal to her family, even though they had mortified her countless times.

A few hours later, Homer came staggering up the highway toward the farm, drunker than a bar full of sailors. He weaved up to mom, vomit drying on his clothes, and mumbled, "Had a li'l assadent downa road." Then he went inside, fell on his bed, and passed out. Homer hadn't turned over a new leaf—he had turned over dad's new pickup. It was totalled. Dad went down and saw it, upside down and smashed, muttered a few cuss words, and then called the wrecker.

That was my old man all the way. He wouldn't lend me his pickup to haul something, but he'd give the keys to a dedicated drunkard and wave bye-bye. I never did say anything about it, but I felt it served him right.

When Homer recovered and was cleaned up, dad gave him a bus ticket and $10, and that was the last we ever saw of him. Years later, I heard he had died in the alcoholics' ward in a Texas VA hospital. That in itself was pretty remarkable, because in World War II, he had served only six months before drinking and brawling got him out of the army on a Section Eight discharge (for undesirable conduct). I was surprised that he qualified for VA benefits.

The more I look back, the more I realize that my dad was a curious man in many ways—like giving to strangers what he wouldn't give to his own family. He provided for us, with mom's help and ours, but he certainly never spoiled us. It took me a long time to realize that maybe this wasn't the worst way. Whether it was or not, it was J. W. Childress's way. Right now, I wish he were alive to read what I'm writing, but since he had already lived it, it probably wouldn't interest him. Like all of us, he preferred praise to criticism and practiced his share of denial.

I'm not sure how much I really loved him, because love is different things to different people. But I do know I respected him, and had affection for him, and would always do anything I could for him. Which I guess I did, because twenty-two years is a long time, even when the folks involved are your parents. True, I lived a life of my own during that time, but I was always at their beck and call.

On the other hand, dad never ran away from his family, or his responsibilities, and he wasn't a boozer—although two of his brothers had trouble with John Barleycorn. One reason dad drank so little was that it took so little to make him drunk. He did drink beer with his fishing buddies but rarely got tipsy.

WHEN I REACHED El Reno, it was midnight, and not even Interstate 40 had much traffic on it. The station was dark, the owner gone home. (By the time I got back home, it would be 5:00 AM—and no, dad didn't offer to buy me breakfast.)

The blue Chrysler, a dark mound, sat beside a telephone booth. I eased up next to it, my tires making quiet chewing sounds on the gravel. Then, just to be ornery, I punched my horn. It was a two-trumpet job and really opened up the night. Dad popped up in the backseat, whacking his head against the roof. I got out, smiling hugely, and opened his door.

"Well, well," I said. "There you go hitting the roof again."

He got out, rubbing his head, and locked the Chrysler. After we were on the road for a few minutes, he said, "I reckon I fell asleep."

"Yeah?" I said. "I didn't have that luxury. I just came off a five-hundred-mile drive when you called mom." He didn't say he was sorry. He never did that in his life. Instead, he sat up in alarm.

"You sure you can drive? You ain't too sleepy?"

I should have said, yes, I was sleepy, and made him drive, but like a dummy, I didn't. "I'm fine," I grumbled. "I drank twenty cups of coffee." Dad pondered that for about a millisecond.

"Good," he said, and leaning against the door, he fell asleep again. He'd remember the Chrysler tomorrow and would want a ride back, but I would say, "Gee, dad, I'm sorry, but I have to go to St. Louis" (315 miles in the other direction). Besides, Greyhound left Anderson daily.

AS I DROVE WEST along Highway 60, headed for Anderson and dad's funeral, a beautiful October sky, pearled with cotton-boll clouds, nearly made me miss the spider rappelling from the sun visor into my lap. He did it with such speed, I saw only a small, fat sphere dropping like a stone. Reflexes take over in such cases, and without thinking I slapped my lap.

There are things that I have regretted in my life, and this was one. The car swerved crazily, but even though I was preoccupied with a cramp the size of Alaska, I managed to steer it safely to the side of the road. There I sat, sweating and taking little breaths like a woman in a Lamaze class until the pain eased. The spider fared better than I did, because I missed him. It was awhile before I could muster enough interest to inquire about his location, but wherever he was, I hoped there wouldn't be a repeat performance.

Spiders have always spooked me, even though as a kid I let them walk on my skin. They're just so doggone ugly. Nature's efficient killing tool—and yet I've often used them in my writing. In college, I took a job as a caretaker on a small ranch. It belonged to a wealthy man who paid me miserly wages ($35 a month) to watch his cows. But as a student, I was glad to have the work, which came with a four-room hut. In any case, the vet came to spray the cows for horn flies, and one of the little critters made it to my window sill, where it buzzed a final sermon about the evils of DDT before dying.

The Fly

I watched a crippled fly as it lay dying
On my sink's edge, in delicate counterpoise
Between life and death, thrusting up its feet
In mute protest towards the firmament.
No sound told me it knew what all this meant
Or that it understood the depth of dying.
A stroke could make of me a god or devil,
Or even both, effect as well as cause,
But each thing has its own eleventh hour,
And so I left it there. When I returned,
I saw the sum of mercy it had earned
With all its supplications and its prayers:
A silken angel, descended from its gauze,

Had come down to minister and devour,
And bore its victim up the silver stairs.

I've often pondered the astonishments of life among the tinier citizens of these hills. They make human living look like child's play. Once in a rusty old fuse box on a pole, I saw where a cockroach lived on the castoffs of a spider—commensalism at its most unique. Another time I saw a spider dart from under the windshield wiper of dad's truck to snare a pair of mating flies—proof that love can be dangerous.

I thought about that rusty old fuse box. I was living in my Ozark trailer then, and my middle son was living with me, as all my sons did from time to time. The spider, plump as a burgher, was pleased with her digs. The gateway to the larder was silk, stretching across a one-inch hole where a fuse had been. The mystery was how she caught enough there to get so fat—why would any insect in its right mind venture into so murderous a cave?

Just then a scurrying movement caught my eye. Another spider? Ah, no, for if two such monks shared the same cell, there would soon be only one monk. But what other insect would dare camp on the estate of so efficient a killer? Again the lightning-swift movement, a brown blur that whipped around a rusty fitting and hid under it. Only one bug moved that fast—*la cucaracha*.

"Jace!"

Jason, then sixteen, was burning trash. "Come look at this, son."

Jason ambled over. "What is it?"

"See that pile of dead insect remnants—wings, legs, and stuff?"

"Sure."

"Well, that spider up there can't eat such rations, but apparently his boarder can."

"What boarder?"

Whizzzz!

"Whoa!" Jason's exclamation told me he'd spotted the cockroach, and we settled down to some serious bug-gazing. We must have presented an odd sight to anyone passing along the road, hunkered over a rusty fuse box, but that was nothing new. The roach lived in a messy house, and obviously the spider wasn't going to be his maid. Bits and pieces of insect corpses littered the old fuse box like a tiny diorama of *The Texas Chain Saw Massacre*. It was an insect Aceldama, a miniature charnel house. And the cockroach was the resident buzzard.

I wondered how they avoided *xenophobia*—fear or suspicion of strangers—a natural human trait. It's why us folks from the deep Ozarks don't want much to do with city people. No matter how fine they look, we're suspicious of them. Unless, of course, they're nice and fat.

These bugs, or what remained of them, had once gone about nature's business without a care in the world. But alas, much of nature's business is conducted by barter—and she thinks nothing of trading one eight-legged bundle of calories to feed some other hungry insect.

DEATH IS the Siamese twin of life. While I'm alive at the moment, I'm perfectly aware that in a year or ten I won't be. But dying is something none of us like to think about. There is such finality to it, we ignore it in hopes it'll go away.

I don't know what death is, but I do know it lasts awhile, and that fact has fueled my philosophy when it comes to enjoying as much of life as I can. My biggest regret is that I can't die and then write a best-seller about it, like those lucky stiffs with their tunnels and pastures of light. The best I can hope for is my own epitaph, engraved on my headstone:

> Well, here I am,
> and guess what?
> No heaven.
> No hell.
> No god.
> No satan.
> No angels.

No demons.
No morons
Claiming there are.

Animals dying natural deaths don't seem to have the problems with it that humans do. Growing up on a farm exposed me early to the deaths of livestock and the disposal of their remains—which, in our impoverished area, was usually left to nature. Ailing cows or horses just wandered off and died, thereby furnishing calories for buzzards, crows, and maggots.

Having led a rough and adventurous life, I've often doubted that I'd die in bed. I got through the Korean War with only a damaged eardrum, escaped drowning in the rapids of Idaho's Snake River, survived thirty-three military mass-parachute jumps, was saved by my mother from burning to death and by my father from an enraged bull, and was recently astonished to see a semitrailer flipping over and catching fire on the freeway ahead of my wife and me. But I hope I have a cordial dying to look forward to, since I have a low pain threshold.

I'm not the only one who is fascinated by our final resolution. Poets have always written about this most natural of events. Death and dying lend themselves to drama better than anything except war, which, of course, is about death and dying. The late novelist William Saroyan and I corresponded for years. I visited him in Fresno and always admired his attitude towards death. Before he died of cancer in 1981 in the VA hospital, he quipped, "Everybody's got to die sometime, but I thought they'd make an exception in my case!"

Unfortunately, death is rarely seen as humorous. Wry, cynical, bitter, plaintive, and tragic—these are more associated with the final fog that rolls over all our harbors. When Mark Twain died, he left a note indicating that he welcomed death as a release from sadness and suffering, of which he had his share. "Death, the only immortal, who treats us all alike, whose peace and refuge are for all, the soiled and the pure, the rich and the poor, the loved and the unloved."

IN MID-1983, dad's heart began to fail. He walked slowly, shuffling his feet, and any strong exertion made him wheeze like a tired old hound. But at sixty-eight, his coal black hair made him look much younger.

I took him to St. Johns Hospital in Joplin, Missouri, for tests, and there, with me standing by, he flunked the treadmill. It was painful to watch him laboring on that artificial hill, grimly plodding forward while a welter of wires told of chaos in his chest. None of his other tests were any good, either. Dr. Joe Graham, a brilliant heart surgeon who had studied with Dr. Michael DeBakey, gave it to him straight.

"Jay, you need a heart bypass operation," he said. "Without it, you're in big trouble."

Joe Graham was a tall, lean Texan whose hobby was raising longhorn cattle. He had a fine herd of these beautiful animals when I knew him. He told me dad might make it another two or three years, but he might not, too. Decades of smoking had severely damaged his heart and lungs.

Dad accepted the news impassively, as he did everything. But later in the car, I could tell he was scared. No one else would have suspected a thing. It was one of those polished-brass days, with sunlight everywhere and birds performing aerial ballets. I wondered what he was thinking and then realized I would never know. When it came to personal problems, my father was a closed book to all who knew him—and for all the years I knew him.

In November 1983, Dr. Graham performed a quintuple bypass on dad's heart that went off without a hitch. Although a typical bypass was often less than a five-way procedure and lasted five to seven years, dad's quintuple operation gave him fourteen more good years—an unusually long time for such surgery in the early 1980s. I remember Dr. Graham saying, "If I had my choice, I'd never perform less than five-way bypasses."

Immediately after his heart surgery, dad didn't care about anything. I took a photograph of him in his hospital bed, when he was coming out of anesthesia, and he looked deader than a pie-eyed mackerel. He was out cold, his mouth was open, and his dentures were God knew where. For some reason, he never did like that picture.

MONTHS LATER, I was crossing the pasture to visit dad on one of those rare evenings when clouds sit like bowls of fruit on the skyline and a setting sun paints them gold. Ozark sunsets are beautiful, and this one was no exception. I turned around and started walking backward, the better to see a sky that had become a cauldron of rippling colors. That was how I tripped over the trailer tongue, went sprawling on my backside, and knocked the wind out of myself.

After a moment, I got up, dusted off, and looked at the culprit— an ancient wooden-framed vehicle (more of a cart, really) with a steel tongue and two rubber tires. It was a homemade job that had sat half-hidden in the pasture's tall grass for so long that the end of the tongue was buried deep in the earth. The tires were still half inflated, but the trailer's wooden bed was rotted from years of weathering. Seeing it there, its green paint faded and flaking, I thought of the days when my family worked fields from Oklahoma to California, picking cotton, cutting broomcorn—whatever the grower required.

Hard, hard work in a hard, hard life.

God, how I remember those times. Hands frozen by the frost on cotton bolls, brains baked by a hundred desert suns, sharing tomatoes or pork and beans from a big can held by mom—our lunch for the day. At sundown, tired beyond belief, we dragged ourselves back to the shack the farmer furnished his migrants, waiting with growling stomachs for whatever mom "rustled up," as she said—often just biscuits and gravy, or pinto beans in a pot that mom, leaving the fields, started simmering at noon.

Being raised the son of a sharecropper had not been to my liking, but as it turned out, it was to my overall good. As it happened, when I joined the army, dad gave up farming and headed for the city—where my siblings were well-behaved country kids no longer. In the city, they couldn't sort cucumbers, peanuts, or watermelons all day to quell their youthful exuberance. So they filled their idle hours by becoming thorns in their parents' backsides. In self-defense, dad married the two girls off when they were hardly out of pinafores. Once David was old enough, he went to work as a carpenter in construction, and he's been there ever since.

The next morning, over the creek-bottom mud he called coffee, I asked dad about the relic I had tripped over in the pasture. He said the trailer, already old when he bought the farm, could have been used by some migrating family—thousands of whom came from Missouri. Where were the people now who had loaded that trailer with dreams, to head for a golden land in pursuit of a rainbow? Did they still exist, and if so, were they still roving? There's often talk about how mobile we've become in America, but actually we've been a nation of fiddle-feet since the end of the Revolutionary War. We wanted to head for the sunset, and the Ozarks' chief city—a muddy little camp called St. Louis—was already a gateway to the West. Everyone headed west back then. Today, though, the West has run out. So we're turning back on ourselves and discovering America all over again. That's how I rediscovered the Ozarks, which I had left as a very young child.

To some folks, old trailers are just pieces of junk, but to me, they're history. Painted by endless desert sunsets, stained by the sweat of people chasing the American dream, they're modern-day Conestogas that have earned the right to rest.

WHEN I WAS WRITING my "Out of the Ozarks" column for the *St. Louis Post-Dispatch,* it was read by folks of every persuasion. Sometimes readers drove all the way to Anderson, way west of St. Louis, and sought out my trailer to say hello. At public appearances, people from all over the Midwest came. One morning a young man pulled in and jumped out of his car waving several sheets of yellow lined paper. "My co-workers tell me this is the funniest thing they ever read!" he hollered. "I'd like to know what you think!"

Forty years of slinging ink has made me realize the utter futility of saying *anything* to would-be writers. Today, especially, because the computer and "software" has made everybody a "writer."

Yeah, right! If my comments aren't what they want to hear, they leave in a huff, after showing up uninvited, without any thought of offering to pay for my services. I'd like to see them try that with a plumber.

As such stuff always is, what the guy gave me was gibberish. His co-workers were either blockheads, or they just wanted to get rid of him. "Why, this is wonderful!" I said, acting excited. "But I'm only a writer, not the final authority. What you need is to send this to an editor as quickly as you can. I would type it first, though."

"What's an editor?"

"An editor is a man or woman who waits for writers to send stuff and then buys it for good money."

"How do I go about that?"

"Go to the post office."

I wrote down the name and address of an editor I didn't like, told my visitor to enclose a stamped, self-addressed return envelope, and sent him on his way.

MY FORTY-ODD YEARS as a writer and poet have afforded me some good laughs over the way regular folks view us typewriter tramps. They seem to think freelance writers are James Bonds with laptops, immersed in glamour and intrigue. But they haven't slept where I have—in a pickup by Billy the Kid's grave on a freezing New Mexico night, or in my car on a snowbound Utah highway, or inside a one-man tent in a snake-infested Mexican desert.

I've come close to the angels for pay that was too low and too slow, from publishers who were stingy and greedy. The hours are long and the wages short when you write for magazines, and being broke is almost a career. Dad was always surprised that I didn't end up in the poorhouse.

"A *writer?*" he said. "You'll never make a goddamn dime! And since you can't farm, you need to find yourself a unionized trade." That kind of talk ended, of course, when he started reading about himself in some of my stories. I could tell he was tickled, but of course he never said so. He liked to needle me.

"I never read those poems you write," he said. "They don't make any sense, and half the time they don't even rhyme. As for your stories, you exaggerate too much." I couldn't get him to understand that real poetry had much more to do with Emily Dickinson than it did with Hallmark, and that biographical writing wasn't reporting. But if he knew I was doing this book, he'd enjoy being spotlighted again. He just wouldn't tell me.

IF I WERE TO DEFINE my parents, I would say they were hard workers whose dreams were defeated at every turn. Dysfunctional to an impressive degree, their lives were riddles they were always trying to solve. But between raising four kids and coping with daily existence, they never really did.

Despite a legion of differences, mom and dad stayed together for fifty-five years, until she died in 1992. Oddly enough, they were married for only fifty-three of those years. Late in their lives, after more than half a century together, my parents divorced. Or rather mom filed for divorce against dad. He didn't want any part of it, and as it would turn out, they started living together again towards the end of their lives—probably because they couldn't live apart. They never remarried, preferring to exist in a kind of disagreeable limbo. The only thing that stopped them from fighting was that they got too old.

But mom kept her pitching arm right up to the end. One day in the mid-1980s, I heard dad hollering my name outside my trailer and stuck my head out to see mom chucking rocks the size of softballs at him as he dodged among the walnut trees.

"You sorry bastard!" she was yelling. "You killed my chickens!"

"Grab her, Bill! I can't do a thing with her!" That was my dad. *Whack!* A rock ricocheted off the tree he was hiding behind. Like an ungainly stork, he galloped to another. *Whop!* Mom nailed that one, too. Where was a baseball scout when you needed one? She even had a good wind-up.

Some of mom's ire could be attributed to menopause, which in her case was a call to war, and some of it resulted from her having a snootful, as on this occasion. Like all of her family, she had poor tolerance for alcohol. It wasn't a problem when she was young, but after her children left and her mental problems began, she started drinking more heavily.

"I'm finding partly full bottles of rye hidden all over the place," dad told me. "In the barn, in the chicken house, even in the cellar. She's okay till she gets on that stuff, then she's impossible to live with." He added, "I never told you this, but she came home snockered more than once when she worked as a housekeeper for those rich folks in 1957. You was in Europe then, as a paratrooper. I think her problem started then. She'd locate their liquor cabinet and by day's end would be feeling no pain. It's a wonder she didn't kill somebody on the highway."

Mom's dead chickens were a family joke, one of dozens of real or imagined grudges that she held against dad. The incident had happened back in 1946 (the rock chucking was in 1989). We were moving from one ramshackle farm to another, for reasons known only to dad. Mom had recently ordered a hundred baby chicks to raise, and they weren't quite pullet-sized by the time we moved. The new place was an hour's drive, by way of a rough dirt-and-gravel road.

Mom objected strongly to dad's loading plan, which was to put the chicks in the back of his high-sided pickup rather than in boxes. But he wore her down, assuring her that these birds were too big to pile up—a fear with young chicks. Unfortunately, the trip in the swaying truck did cause the poultry to pile up, and they smothered by the dozen. It was dad's fault, no doubt about it.

I can still hear mom's agonized wail when they dropped the tailgate and saw a mound of melted chickens. They started pulling out the dead birds, and with every one, mom let out an "Oh, my *God!*" They lost about seventy of the chicks, and for the next forty years, the event was one of mom's launching pads for invective against dad. She forgave him for some things, but not for murdering her chickens.

In spite of these excitements, they stayed together until the end. And when cancer, like some hideous spider, slowly dragged mom towards eternity, dad cared for her as tenderly as he would a baby. He was then seventy-seven and nowhere near as strong as he once was, but he wouldn't put mom in a nursing home until he could no longer care for her. Even then, the nursing home was only a couple of miles away, and he spent many hours at her bedside, as I did. Several times when she was still lucid, I brought my twelve-string guitar and sang her favorite song, "Danny Boy."

From two hundred and thirty pounds, mom shrank to less than a hundred pounds at death, knew nothing of what went on around her, and babbled senseless phrases. She had ceased to be the woman who gave me life and was now death's personal trophy. In her casket, when she finally died, she looked like a little gray-haired child. And in the end, she went to her rest rejecting preachers and religion, even though—perhaps like most of us—she had once tried that impossible road.

But love rarely has much to do with religion. Religion today is more related to politics—perhaps has always been. So, what kept my folks together, in spite of their many battles and personal failures? I think they finally realized that celestial rabbits-feet didn't work. Towards the end of their lives, they learned to live their lives and not rely on crutches; not religion, not drugs, and not the likes of Charles Manson, Jim Jones, or David Koresh and his Waco wackos.

Uncle Jack, ever the Childress wit, remarked during a visit when mom and dad were exchanging salvos, "You know as well as I do, Bill, that Jay and Lorraine can't live apart. They need each other to fight with!"

But I think there's another reason. I think our parents made it all those years because dad, in his own strange way, loved his sad, unhappy wife and did his best with what she forever considered herself to be: damaged goods. Nobility is found in strange places, and in their lives, they both knew noble moments.

Whatever those who knew them think, or whatever their children believe, the truth is they raised four kids without a murderer among them and watched them scatter to the four winds. They never meddled after that, just let us struggle to find our own way—

as eventually we did. Not without some bad decisions and danger; but we found it.

I've always been grateful that our parents didn't spoil us rotten, that they tanned our hides if we needed it, and that when our parents spoke, we jumped. Too many times today, it's the parents who jump when the kids speak—reversing thousands of years of successful child-rearing on the say-so of "experts." As one British dignitary said on a U.S. visit, "The thing that impresses me most is the way American parents obey their children."

Dr. Spock, who lived fifty miles from my Ozarks acres, agreed that spanking, properly administered, did more good than harm. Why wouldn't it? It's a kid's first encounter with some kind of government. And governments, like them or not, are the glue that holds civilization together. But this is an emotional issue, and when it comes to corporal punishment, hardly anyone is as opposed to it as America's post–baby boom moms.

Not my mom, though. She could and did administer punishment, but she also knew it had more lasting impact if she said, "Your dad will be done plowing soon, and I'll let him decide." That way we were punished all day, waiting for him to come home, because we knew dad could be relied on to do his duty with vigor. Many years later, after my own (occasionally spanked) sons were grown and doing fine, dad and I talked about this.

"I never liked paddling you kids," he said. "I only did it when you'd done something that could be bad for others. Playing with matches, for instance.

"A lot of educated people are against corporal punishment," he continued as we sat under an oak tree in his yard. "They've spent the last forty years hollering about it. But if those who favor physical punishment don't have the answers, neither do those who don't. It's like the death penalty—they can call up statistics to support either argument, but one thing is for sure, the gas chamber keeps serial killers and rapists from murdering somebody else, and a lack of it don't. The punishment you kids earned taught you the value of obeying rules—and that's not a bad thing to know."

AS A MAN BLESSED with good health most of my life, aging has been a shock. I even thought about writing a diary of the aging process—the rights, wrongs, and in-betweens of a human body beginning to flag, drag, and sag. Dad once said the real curse of old age is that the body fails before the mind does. "Your mind tells your body that it's still eighteen," he said. "Then you test it, and your body says, 'Not hardly!'" Toward the end, he wouldn't even take a daily walk. His legs were weak, and he was afraid he'd fall. He sat in his chair with his cat on his lap and watched baseball.

During our good later years, dad and I zinged each other a lot, teasing constantly. "You're not walking these days," I might chide him. "I guess that means you're getting old."

"So are you," he would retort. "Ain't nobody escaped it yet."

"Maybe if you exercised more, you wouldn't be so ugly."

"Maybe if you didn't talk so much, I wouldn't have a headache."

Soon after I turned sixty-three, my VA doctor had some unsettling news for me. "You're Type II diabetic," she said. "And you have high blood pressure."

"Why?" I was dumbfounded.

She smiled wryly. Aging was starting to happen to her, too. "In general, for most folks, it's just part of getting older." I always liked that doctor. She told the truth, the simple facts, and didn't toss a lot of powdered sugar on the French toast.

I began to experience other parts of the aging process, too, and with each one, a new adventure. Like the time I had a little number called *plantar fasciitis*, where my inner foot separated from the bone—or something like that. For two months, I could barely hobble, so severe was the pain. My HMO wouldn't do anything about it, either. "It'll heal itself," I was told. "It just takes time."

"How much time?"

"Four months."

Today the foot has regrown itself (or whatever it did) and is just fine. But being unable to walk for such a long period made me happy that I make my living not by standing but by sitting.

A nineteenth-century writer named Henri Amiel put it this way:

"Knowing how to grow old is the masterwork of wisdom, and one of the most difficult chapters in the great art of living." But I like what actress Bette Davis said: "Old age is no place for sissies!"

THE TOYOTA TOPPED A RISE, and in front of me, down a long sloping hill, lay Granby. It's one of Missouri's oldest mining towns, and on this late afternoon in October, it was picture-perfect with its venerable water tower and the buildings along the main street that its citizens have worked to restore. I stop for gas and gossip—but, of course, I get none of the latter because the attendant knows I'm not local.

"Nice day," I said.

"Ain't it, though."

"Anything happening in Granby?" The reporter's instinct dies hard.

"Nothin' ever happens in Granby."

"You live here, then?"

"Not me. I live in Diamond."

"Then how do you know nothing ever happens in Granby?"

"*Everybody* knows nothin' ever happens in Granby."

The city of Neosho is only a few miles ahead, and evening's approach is turning the sky parrot-blue. Changing daylight makes me feel like the car is a rocket ship, sliding at great speed into the unknown. The Toyota's space-age instrument panel aids the illusion. Highway 60 has always been a favorite route of mine. During my years in the Ozarks, I drove it many times.

Off to the left, a clump of Holsteins makes Rorschach images on a hill, and crows fight over property rights in a big oak. Few things can beat rural Missouri for beauty, especially in the fall. One of the great riddles of humanity is that we flee the city for the country and then turn the country into the city. Developers can't wait to make each newly discovered outdoor Eden into a multitude of malls.

Before returning to southwestern Missouri, I had phoned the Neosho Chamber of Commerce, which once (and only once) hired me as a speaker. I got a giggly lady who cheered me immeasurably just by being giggly. I asked if anything new had happened in Neosho in the past few years.

"Oh, my, yes! *(Giggle.)* We have a new theater—six screens! And a Wal-Mart Supercenter! *(Giggle.)* And we have forty-eight industries, and Neosho's population is now ten thousand!"

"There used to be a beautiful little park with a brook."

"Oh, yes! Neosho City Park!"

"And it had a big clock on the ground, made out of flowers."

"Oh, yes! *(Giggle.)* A lovely clock!"

"It wasn't working five years ago. How about now?"

"Well, no, darn it, it's not. But it will be! We had a meeting about that just today, and *(giggle)* we're going to *fix that clock!*"

FROM NEOSHO, I head south on Highway 71 toward Anderson, in McDonald County. On my right is Wal-Mart, but the area has ballooned with other businesses, too. A few miles down the road, near old Camp Crowder, there's now a movie theater. I'm glad to see new theaters opening up—but it may spell doom for Anderson's venerable old movie house, The Flick, whose doors have rarely been closed since it first opened in 1939. The McCrackens owned it during my years in and around Anderson, and I saw a lot of good movies there.

But times change, no matter who you are or where you live, and they were changing in Anderson, Noel, and all the little hamlets long before I retired and left for California. Many green-card Mexicans had been hired by the poultry companies, and they, too, were having an impact. There was also more fecal pollution in the local streams, according to the *Grove Sun*, than there was when I first came to southwestern Missouri, and that's bad for tourism. Another eyesore was the shacky, worn-out trailers, bought for a song by quick-buck landlords, dotting the hills around Anderson and Noel to make slum-type homes for the Mexican workers. As a former migrant worker, I knew that story well.

But even though he had spent years in migrant shacks, it didn't bother my dad. "Them trailers are better'n anything they got in Mexico," he said.

MY DAD pretty much lived and died on his own terms, a stubborn patriarch who raised his children to respect and obey him—and the formula never failed. He never came to us about anything. He expected us to come to him. On the other hand, he didn't always care if we did or not—or if he did, he never showed it. He was aloof and a mystery for most of our lives. But he never had to yell at us. He could just turn those blue eyes on us, and we would attack the next job like beavers in a grove of saplings.

For dad's eighty-first birthday in December 1996, all his far-flung kids managed to be there. Dad was proud, even cocky. He had begun to be less reserved and talk a little more as he reached advanced age. "By God, I didn't think I'd live to be eighty-one!" he chuckled. "Ain't ever'body gets to be that old."

"You wouldn't have, either," I said, "if it hadn't been for that heart bypass thirteen years ago."

My oldest sister, Glenda, begged him to come and live with her in Los Angeles's warmer climate, but he refused. His heart was in the Ozarks, always had been, and always would be. "I'll buy you a plane ticket, dad," she pleaded. "We've got everything you need out here!"

"I've got everything I need here," he retorted, "and without the earthquakes. Besides, I ain't gittin' on no damn plane." Plenty of people are afraid to fly, and dad was one. But I had to laugh about the earthquakes.

"You're worried about *California* quakes?" I asked. "The biggest one in U.S. history happened right here in Missouri."

"No, it didn't," he replied.

"Yes it did," I persisted. "It made the Mississippi run backwards. It's in the history books, if you'd ever read anything but Louis L'Amour westerns."

"Baloney." He was just that way, adamant and stubborn with his kids, who weren't allowed to know more than their elders. Strangely enough, he was never like that with others, preferring to be silent and rarely venture an opinion.

"I'll bet twenty bucks you're wrong," I said.

"I don't want to take your money."

"You won't," I promised. "And I'll expect you to pay up when I win."

"You ain't gonna win."

So I located the information about the New Madrid earthquake of 1811, and next time I saw him, I read it to him. I already knew I was right. I'd written a newspaper story about it and showed him the clipping.

"Twenty bucks," I said smugly.

"That don't prove nothin'. For all I know, you had that news-paper printed at one of those fake places."

I won all my bets with dad but never collected. He didn't pay bets he made with his kids. He'd told me I'd lose, and he made sure of it. It was sometime before I realized that this was his idea of a practical joke, and he got a big kick out of it. He would get me all wrought up about some piece of knowledge, knowing I was a smart aleck by nature, and then lower the boom. It was his way of say-ing, "You may have seven years of college, but I have seventy years of living."

SIX MONTHS BEFORE dad's death, after twenty-four years in those ancient hills, I finally left the Ozarks. I'd been at his beck and call for over two decades except when I was on the road. Now mom was five years gone, and at sixty-four, I had made up my mind to leave. It wasn't a happy decision.

One day I said, "Dad, I'm just an old man looking after an older man. You've got everything you need here, and you'll never have to live in a rest home. But I'm sixty-four, and whatever years I have left, I want for me. I've been writing to a woman in California, a pen pal, and she wants me to come and visit her. Besides, I'm as close as the telephone. I'll call you weekly, and all of us kids will still come and visit." So impassive was he, he could have been a wooden Indian. I swear, he even looked like the chief on that old Indian head nickel.

Dad was strong for his modest size. I once saw him lift a two-hundred-pound log, walking it up and then lowering it onto his shoulder to carry it. He also wore clothes well and looked great when all dressed up in gabardine slacks and a white Stetson—his favorite going-to-town garb. Mostly though, he wore jeans or overalls.

Of course, when dad lost his temper he could thunder with the best of them. He had a way of folding his tongue between his teeth when he was about to explode. When his blue eyes sparked fire, we kids knew death was near and lit out for the south forty. As a result of this acting gift, he didn't have to resort to corporal punishment as much as lesser fathers did. He could quell us with a single look.

Another Spartan trait was that dad never complained about life, even at its toughest. However, it always surprised me that he could stand more pain around strangers than he could around his own family. At home, a mashed thumb would mobilize a whole army of profanity. But if he cut off a foot in front of someone he didn't know, he would probably say, "I wonder if you could find me a Band-aid?"

Now, as I told him I was about to leave, he fixed me with those blue eyes that so contrasted with his black hair and said, "Well, you got to do whatever you think is right."

No emotion, no anger, no visible reaction. Life had taught him the futility of argument in such matters. People would do what people would do—even as he himself had done. We said our good-byes like the geezers we had become, and I left for California. There, six months later, I got word of his death. I never found out until after he died that soon after I left, dad told one of his friends, "I'm sure gonna miss him."

It took him over twenty years to say that, and even then he didn't say it to me. That was my dad. When it came to anything personal, he was always a day late and a dollar short. He never acknowledged anything I did, even in childhood. He never gave mom a compliment about her cooking or the way she looked. He was an emotional vacuum who never praised his kids, but who would tell others what he thought, knowing it would get back to us. His life was built on sternness and stoicism, the shields that protected him from hurt.

He never saw the need for singing anyone's praises, yet he risked his life to save mine.

Mom did the same. There was never any question of their love. They just didn't show it in the effusive guaranteed-to-spoil-kids way parents do today. Our parents proved it by keeping us safe, fed, and clothed in a world of tough times and mean places. The greatest tribute I can give to their child-rearing practices was that they steered us past many obstacles, keeping us safe until we were grown and could fend for ourselves. Kid-glove treatment wasn't in their lexicon, but they weren't mean—they were responsible. If one of us did something wrong, we were punished, and although we would have preferred mom (mothers being pushovers for kids), we invariably got dad. It's no joke to say I can still feel the burn from those sessions. To this day, though, I'm convinced they helped all of us kids to grow up and be decent citizens.

I REACHED ANDERSON LATE in the day, turning off Highway 71 onto Highway 59, which connected with Main Street. Main Street looked much the same, dowdy but dear, a cluttered tunnel of building-and-tree-lined asphalt ending at the town water tank on the next hill. Anderson occupied a small valley lined by businesses of every description, including the feed mill, which squatted like a cement spider by the railroad tracks.

The ugly skeleton of that dust-polluting feed mill announces Anderson to the world. For most of my sojourn in this tiny Ozark town, I hated that mill—the more so since I lived virtually under it for five years, often waking to find grain-dust covering my car. Who knows what it's done to people's lungs over the long haul?

Local politics wrenched the mill into place years ago, on the premise that it would help the town prosper. All it did was help the owners prosper and create a civic eyesore. Soon after it was built, one disgruntled citizen scaled the hundred-foot tower and, with a rope sling, hung head-down from the top to spray-paint his views. Next morning in big black letters, the outraged owners were treated to the message: SEX, DRUGS, ROCK & ROLL! Now, this was heavy-duty for a town with a dozen churches and no bars, and I believe the artist spent some time in the local jail for his sentiments. But he was a shining knight, a kicker of rich shins—at least for awhile.

When I lived in Anderson, I was once approached by a gentleman, a former banker, who knew I traveled a lot and wanted me to suggest ways that Anderson could attract tourism. I was glad he had come to an expert and gave him my best advice.

"Build a giant chicken," I said. "Anderson is near the chicken and egg center of the world, and people love being part of something big. You could have a poultry library in the bottom, a café at the top, and get the Egg Lady of Columbia to christen the place."

Not only did he not applaud my idea, he laughed at it. And yet, he was perfectly peaceful about that ugly feed mill. Maybe that's because it was reportedly built by one of the county's richest, most self-important cow barons, a fellow who once kited checks through his own bank. That crime was written up in the *St. Louis Post-Dispatch*. Anyway, when the kiting case went to trial, it was nearing Christmas, and the gentle judge in the case let the crook bypass jail, ordering him instead to distribute $100,000 worth of holiday food to St. Louis's needy. I never heard if he did, but I have my doubts. He was a greedy bastard.

That "gentleman" was descended from some of those pioneers I mentioned. I used to wonder what others of similar ilk did— they couldn't all kite checks. Being new in town and ignorant of its history, I wondered about their claims to fame, so I asked a local historian.

"What have these folks done?" I asked.

"Done?" she said. "They don't have to do anything. Their forebears were early arrivals here and built the town."

"You mean they dug the foundations and laid the bricks?"

"Well, not exactly, they had slaves to do that."

"Well, then, have they written any poems, plays, or books or invented anything significant? Perhaps some of them composed songs, painted pictures, or held public office?"

"Goodness! How inquisitive you are! I don't think they have, I haven't heard of anything like that, but they are certainly important people, because their ancestors got here first. I should think that would be quite enough, sir!"

"It's more than enough," I said. "It's a privilege to be allowed to admire their accomplishments."

Some people don't agree with my idea that pioneers should be automatically admired. A proud descendant of an old Anderson family once strutted into a local liquor store, picked out several bottles, and told the new owner, "Just put this on ———'s bill."

"Sorry, no credit," said the new owner, an outspoken blond woman from California who told me the story.

"I guess you don't know who I am?" snapped the customer.

"I guess I don't *care* who you are," said the owner. "No credit!" That particular customer was accustomed to being catered to all over town, so it must have been a shock.

I DIDN'T STOP at the Ozark Funeral Home in Anderson, where the shell that once held my father waited in its last tiny apartment. I'd first join my sisters and brother, who would be driving in from the Tulsa Airport to Grove, Oklahoma, where dad's trailer sat beside Grand Lake o' the Cherokees.

I passed the Main Street mural (which I recommend to visitors who want to gaze on Anderson's Family Tree), then turned right onto Highway 60. The final glow of sunset was just beginning. How many sunsets had I seen during my decades in the Ozarks? Thousands, perhaps, and never once grew tired of them. As I aimed the car towards Oklahoma, massive clouds boiled up, then turned blacker than a fiddle case. An icy wind forced me to roll up the windows, but then, as if having some cumulonimbus afterthought, the clouds rose swiftly higher and began drifting past, looking almost friendly.

No tornadoes this time, and that was fine with me. I was now technically on the fringes of the infamous Tornado Alley, but the Ozarks are seldom targets of tornadoes. The closest may have been one that narrowly missed my trailer in 1978 and then went on to hit Neosho and flatten a motel. On that day, I put my three sons under a mattress and hoped for the best. Luckily, we weren't hit. Mobile homes really get mobile in tornadoes.

AS THE TOYOTA PURRED westward out of Anderson, the skyline below the clouds turned amber and green, a brooding tapestry that brought me inner peace—I didn't know why. Changing skies do that for me. Then a curious thing happened, and I pulled the car to the side of the road to watch.

A hole was slowly swirling into shape on the horizon, a greenish bronze whirlpool. Clouds ruled most of the heavens, but on the skyline the sun was fighting for its right to shine. First, the fiery circle had to conquer a band of low clouds, which refracted light upwards like a spout of water vapor. The sky was lined with a pearly luster. It was like the whole firmament was supported by a golden pillar, and I sat transfixed, lost in the beauty of the sight, before driving on towards Grove.

Ozark nights have always been special to me. They're like a midnight laundry that prepares the hills for the next sunrise. Half an hour later, I turned into the road leading towards Grand Lake. I drove slowly, windows open, taking in the homes, trailers, and night lights. A cool wind was blowing, making the trees creak and tossing a few bats around like falling leaves. Few things can beat an autumn night with breezes stirring, the smells of fallen leaves, and the sounds of creatures, large and small, roving through the woods. Or the vibrations of frogs striking up a band by some pond or stream as the music of insects pours from their tiny worlds. A mercury lamp atop a light pole, made flickery by the parachuting leaves, cast golden eyes on the side of a church, like the revolving mirror-ball at some long-ago dance hall.

In the brightness of daylight, I had kept my father's death at a distance. Now, the reality of why I was here was closing in. There was a tightness in my chest. I would never see him alive again, never tease him, never remind him of things he'd rather forget—and sometimes denied. Never know how a man could reach his eighties and still have undyed black hair. Maybe that's why mom labeled him "black Dutch." Or she might have had some other motive in mind.

I thought about the knowledge, skills, and experience that had vanished, along with the bad habits like smoking and chewing tobacco. I remembered the deep laugh and resonant voice he kept to the end—an end made certain by emphysema. Dad quit smoking before his heart bypass, but it was too late to make any difference. He still craved nicotine, so he chewed Copenhagen—the snuff all those honorable athletes endorse and influence our kids to use. Dad died while reaching for his oxygen bottle.

EPILOGUE

I PASSED DAD'S TRAILER, deciding on a last look at the 1890 church built by Mathias Splitlog, a fabulously wealthy Indian who built his own railroad from Kansas City to Grove. The Splitlog name still graced buildings and cemeteries in Oklahoma and Missouri, and Mathias was buried with his family in the cemetery beside Splitlog Church. Another Splitlog Cemetery existed in Anderson, and it would be my parents' final resting place.

A strange and wonderful light was seeping into the cemetery. I looked east over Grand Lake, past the old steepled church. A moon like a pirate's gold doubloon was creeping over the trees. Soon it would hang in a velvet-blue sky, a medallion suspended from the throat of heaven.

Dad probably never thought about full moons. He loved the lake because he loved to fish, which was why he'd chosen this place to retire. Here was where he lived his final years, and here he died. What Oklahoma ever brought him but pain and tragedy I don't know, but he must have found something.

A cool wind rippled the lake as I turned around and drove to dad's trailer. The moon had become a silver chariot wheel surrounded by stars—scattered candles in the cathedral of night. My headlights struck dad's old steel chair where he read western novels and fed stray animals, a skinny old man in house slippers, his face remarkably unlined for a man of almost eighty-two.

My brother David and sister Glenda had already arrived. Their rental cars were parked next to the trailer. Helen and John's trailer sat in a low place about one hundred feet north of dad's.

How strange and wonderful life is. How full of risks and brimming with rewards. I've never known anyone who said their life turned out the way they thought it would, or even wanted it to, and yet we continue to have impossible dreams. What would we be without them? They cost nothing, and sometimes we awaken to treasures that cannot be counted. "I, being poor, have only my dreams," wrote the poet William Butler Yeats. I was luckier than that. More of my dreams came true than I could ever have imagined.

IN 1992, mom died peacefully and painlessly from a brain tumor, and in 1997, dad died in his home. Both lived long, eventful lives, seeing more wonders and tragedies than either would have thought possible. But that knowledge came to them only in the looking-back time, when they were old and their lives were winding down. Only then did they have time to sift through the years and recall the treasures. They were too busy living the rest of the time.

Now, years later, I can still picture the giant oaks, the rickety old barn, and the weathered farmhouse. Thirty years inside its walls. That's how long my parents lived there. The house almost killed my dad—or rather, one of its denizens did. Taking down a shirt from an upstairs closet, one he hadn't worn in months, he slipped his arm into a sleeve and was bitten by a brown recluse—a spider far more venomous than a black widow. He nearly died, and he carried to his grave a huge scar under his arm where the venom had rotted away the muscle.

But otherwise, it was a welcoming old house, with a yard so big, quail trotted brazenly across it to rob the chickens of their feed. I saw mom's zinnias growing by the door and her shiny array of jars in the cellar—for she never ceased to can as long as she was able. Mom controlled her demons through sheer hard work.

She ended her life as gutsily as she lived it. Like the sister who died of cancer, she had tried religion, and it hadn't worked. According to the funeral director, she was adamant about her last wishes. "No church crap," she said. "And no damned preacher. Just say a few words yourself. That's all." So the funeral director read a paragraph about her life, and the next stop was the cemetery. It was essentially the same for dad. After eighty years of living in a world filled with chaos and pain, I don't think either of them could quite believe in another hell somewhere else.

LIGHTS ARE SHINING inside the trailer. My brother and sisters are seated around the kitchen table. For some reason, as I open the door under a diamond-dusted sky, images of long ago flicker through my mind—memories of the day I came back home after running away. For a moment, I seem to smell the acrid odor of the cotton fields.

My brother and sisters had played only a small part in my life since then, and I in theirs. We had gone our separate ways. And yet sometimes, even now, I recall scenes of childhood—washing dishes and quarreling at the sink with Glenda. Chasing my little brother David back home crying, from wherever my pals and I were going, and wishing I hadn't. Watching Helen, always a little daredevil, do some crazy stunt. I loved them then, and I love them now. But like so many siblings, we do better with distance between us. California, Idaho, and Tennessee are all represented here tonight.

I knew what I was going to say when I entered. I wouldn't mumble it this time, like I had that long-ago day in Texas. I opened the squeaky screen door and stepped in. My siblings glanced up. We stared at each other across the desert of years.

"I'm back," I said.

WILLIAM CHILDRESS has been a Pulitzer-nominated newspaper columnist, a humorous lecturer, and a folk music performer. A graduate of the Iowa Writers Workshop, he has published thousands of articles, poems, and short stories and five books, including *Out of the Ozarks*. His upcoming books are "Working Man's War" (a memoir), "The Taro Leaf Murders," and "24 Years in Hillbilly Heaven" (ending his Ozark trilogy). He is a magazine writer and photographer and lives in California with his wife and two dogs named Bonnie and Clyde.